CHINESE ZEN
A PATH TO PEACE AND HAPPINESS

CHINESE ZEN
A PATH TO PEACE AND HAPPINESS

WU YANSHENG
TRANSLATED BY TONY BLISHEN

Better Link Press

Outwardly, to be apart from the appearance of things is called Zen; to have no inward confusion is called being concentrated.

—*Platform Sutra*

Contents

Translator's Foreword

When I started this translation of Professor Wu Yansheng's popular book, I was aware of Zen but largely ignorant of it. When I had finished it, I was a little less ignorant and rather more aware.

The difficulties and rewards of the act of translation are determined as much by the subject matter as by the skills, or lack of them, of the translator. At one end of the spectrum it can be merely mechanical, at the other the subject matter can make intellectual and sometimes spiritual demands that require an effort of empathy that brings its own reward.

Professor Wu's book, based on a concern for individual happiness in a rapidly changing society, was aimed at a readership within China that is part of a tradition of spiritual enquiry that has survived for over a thousand years and continues to flourish today. It was written with certain assumptions about the cultural background of the reader in mind. But it was also written to inform, enthuse, and guide. In part it is hortatory and reflects aspects of contemporary life in China, and in the West too.

There is one phrase which occurs again and again throughout the book. This is "*ben xin ben xing.*" I have translated it as "original mind, true character"—the inner self. It is what there was of our spiritual identity before all else and which still exists. It is an essential component of the structure of Zen and demands attention.

This English edition stands by itself. But for those interested in further reading there is a rich field in English from which to choose. I have found the works of the great scholar of Buddhism, D. T. Suzuki, invaluable, particularly his Introduction to Zen Buddhism first published in 1934. More recently, Red Pine's lucid translation and commentary on Hui Neng's *Platform Sutra*, one of the foundation stones of Chinese Zen, is a fine guide to its spiritual and linguistic complexities. Many of the translations of the Buddhist sutras prepared by the Buddhist Text Translation Society are also available online as is Philip Yampolsky's 1967 translation of the Dunhuang version of the *Platform Sutra*. There is also a multitude of websites, in Chinese, Japanese and English, that deal with all aspects of Chinese Zen and Buddhism generally. I have used many of them including A. Charles Muller's excellent Digital Dictionary of Buddhism.

The Chinese text which forms the basis of this translation was prepared by Miss Zhang Yicong from Professor Wu's original text, published in China in 2008. This is the fifth book on which we have co-operated and I am more than ever grateful to her and her colleague Miss Yang Xiaohe for their help and editorial guidance. My debt of gratitude to Diane Davies, who designed the cover and edited the draft translations, increases book by book.

Tony Blishen

Preface

The contents of this book are about Zen. Zen is performed in the sitting position, is achieved through the action of walking and through comprehension and description.

What is Zen when we say it is performed in the sitting position? "Seated alone on a mountain top"—at the summit of a mountain, at the very peak of wonder, at the crest of the enlightenment of one's life, in conversation with the real self, where the body is free of the mind and the mind free of the body. When the leaves wither on the tree, its true form appears. This kind of meditation reveals enlightenment itself.

Zen is realised through the act of walking. The ancient Zen monks took up their alms bowls and travelled alone through the seasons. Their straw sandals trod the clouded peaks and penetrated the mountains and rivers. They scooped up the watery moon in their hands and their robes acquired the fragrance of flowers. Amongst the spring flowers and beneath the autumn moon, in summer cloud and winter snow they came to experience the eternity of each blossom and of each world, the eternity of every petal and every *bodhi* of enlightenment.

Zen is realised through enlightenment. Through the Sakyamuni Buddha holding out the flower and Mahakasyapa smiling in return, Zen has been transmitted generation by generation, through the mists of poetry, through the impression of mind upon mind and the light of lamp upon lamp. The Zen masters, through the raising of an eyebrow, the gesture of a fist or through cold contemplation upon a straw mat, banished all causes and having emptied all away, achieved a sudden flowering of the mind and a flash of enlightenment that revealed all in its true shape and color.

Zen is also described and expounded. However, once Buddhist thought and the concentration of spirit of Zen (*samadhi*) are described in language they easily degenerate into a kind of colloquial currency. Because of this Zen masters have always been reluctant to give easy explanations and preferred the pupil to reach his own understanding. Nevertheless, to help people understand the subtleties and essence of Zen they have never opposed the use of language to demonstrate that which is without language or to give form to that which is without trace, like using a finger to indicate the moon in order to achieve the ultimate essence of things through the wisdom of the printed word.

True nature, attachment, casting away and homecoming are the guiding principles of Buddhism and the threads that run through this book.

The ultimate aim of Zen Buddhism is to allow every living being to achieve both knowledge of its true nature and the enlightenment of its true nature. Zen through meditation, through the act of walking, through enlightenment and through exposition is all a means to this end.

In its childhood mankind is at one with the world that it inhabits. The raised eyebrow, the wink, the scowl or smile are entirely natural. But with the birth of individual knowledge people become separated from this unity with the world and seek fame and profit, pursue pleasure and avoid suffering and hurry towards a life lived in the moment. Then, on life's journey, they are surrounded by exhausted travellers and they ask the heavens in despair:

"Who am I?"

The search for one's true nature is the ultimate concern of Zen. To regain one's original appearance, to return to the absolute realm that existed before the birth of relative knowledge is the main aim of Zen. One's original appearance is the pure self, the true nature of the inner self.

Long ago one of my elders quoted a poem to me:

> Eight measures of talent suffice treasure enough,
> To take a journey of 10,000 *li*[1] across river and hill.

With this encouragement I began to concentrate on that long journey and through the hills and rivers of Zen and beneath the silent lonely light of the moon of my mind I came to realise the realm of Zen.

In this way, both famous and out of the way hills and temples, deep woods and simple shelters were all left with my shadow in its straw sandals and bamboo rain hat seeking the path to enlightenment and meditating in the lotus position.

As I meditated and as I walked and understood, layer by layer my body and spirit dropped away so that finally I had "neither eyes, nor ears, nor mouth, nor nose, nor

---

[1]The *li* is a traditional Chinese unit of distance. 1 *li* equals 0.5 km.

body nor thought," bodiless, like a single drop of water dissolved in the sea.

I became the spring flower and the autumn moon, the summer wind and the winter snow. I became the drops of water on the eaves and the breeze between the pines...

Emptiness was scattered, the land disappeared.

The mountains had no beginning, the bitter cold knew not its year.

In the deep silence the lotus flower of enlightenment blossomed like a jewel.

Zen, with its condensation of Eastern wisdom, its concern for individual life and spirit and the quest for a true life has had a strong effect throughout the world.

Zen is one of the masterpieces of Chinese culture. For a thousand years Zen has integrated with the spiritual life of the literati and scholar officials and lent their lives an air of elegant detachment. Through them Zen has had a deep and long-lasting influence on all aspects of Chinese culture.

From the 12th century onwards Chinese Zen was transmitted to Japan where it was considerably developed and permeated the depths of every level of Japanese life and society to become one of the pillars of Japanese culture itself.

At the beginning of the 20th century Zen was transmitted to Europe and America where it caused a blending of Eastern and Western culture at the deepest spiritual level and pervaded all spheres of Western culture.

The wisdom of Zen empties away a life of quarrelling over profit and desire into a clear spring that washes away all anxiety. The essence of Zen is a direct and effective path for the people of today to grow in wisdom and understanding.

My hope is that through this book people will be able to realize the essentials of Zen and master its essence; stimulate the potential of life and preserve its wisdom; make it more natural, more stable, happier and more tranquil thereby returning to their true nature and living poetically in the world that we inhabit.

Wu Yansheng
At the Zen Residence of Mountain and Water
Xi'an, China
November 2008

Chapter I
The Door to Zen

The Japanese word Zen comes from the Chinese *chan na*, a transliteration of a Sanskrit word meaning "calm thought," "cultivation of the way of thinking" and "assimilating concepts." In other words meditation, the concentration of thought in one place and the consideration of the truths of life through the training of seated Zen so that the impurities of the brain are precipitated and one's thinking becomes as limpid and translucent as water.

Put simply in modern terms, Zen is a realm and a method and a home.

Firstly, Zen is a kind of realm, a realm of awareness, remote from distinctions and the dualism of opposites. In the Zen view of the world everything, organic and inorganic, though it may appear to be different is inherently equal.

Next, Zen is a method, a method for stimulating wisdom. Zen uses "the one and only way" to make us throw off the fetters of distinctions and show the "virtuous aspect of the wisdom of Buddha" that is inherent in all sentient beings.

Thirdly, Zen is a kind of home. Though other places may be fine, nothing is better than going home early. The enlightenment of Zen is like the return of the wandering son. Zen provides a comfortable final destination for the rootless wanderer of the present age and returns us to the spiritual origin of the time before the distinctions between host and guest. The masters of Zen have sought, through many languages and stimuli to make us cease our roaming and return to our spiritual home.

Hui Neng (638 – 713), the Sixth Patriarch of Zen Buddhism in China said in the *Platform Sutra*:

> Outwardly, to be apart from the appearance
> of things is called Zen; to have no inward confusion
> is called being concentrated.

If we can transcend both form and appearance and can remain unmoved amongst the brilliant and seductive colors of the outward world, that is Zen; if, in transcending external form and appearance we can maintain independence of spirit, then that is "being concentrated." Meditative concentration can bring great changes in our outlook on life.

Zen is one of the most effective means for easing the pressures of modern life, of strengthening determination and of opening up to wisdom.

Reducing pressure: The pace of society today makes people's lives hurried, exhausting or even depressed. Zen can ease this pressure and transform it into a motive force.

Reinforcing concentration: When faced with the world of glitter and in the face of all kinds of temptation Zen can give us self-control, adjust our psychological state for the better, allow us to focus our attention, strengthen our meditative concentration and secure us a tranquil, serene, comfortable and happy mental experience.

Opening up to wisdom: There is no wisdom in backbiting and squabbling or mutual deception in the seeking of petty advantage. That is merely low cunning. Zen enables us to open a fundamental wisdom from life's deepest levels that gives us a clear and penetrating vision of universal life.

Clear The Mind and See One's Original Nature

The perceptions gained by Sakyamuni Buddha, the founder

of Buddhism, at the time of his awakening to the way are the ultimate concern of Buddhism. He said:

> All sentient beings possess the virtuous aspect of the wisdom of Buddha but because of vainly held delusions cannot achieve it.

The goal of Zen is to awaken the inherent Buddha nature that is hidden within each one of us so as to achieve a life of awareness, fulfilment and self-confidence.

Holding the Flower and Smiling

A beautiful story is told of the first appearance of Zen Buddhism. It goes that just as Sakyamuni Buddha was preparing to expound the law at the Meeting at Mount Lingshan, the king of the Brahman heaven, one of the protecting deities of the Buddhist law, appeared before the dais, held out a golden *boluo* flower in greeting and then took a seat at the side. The Sakyamuni Buddha took the flower and sat there serenely without saying a word. It is said that very many people came to hear the Sakyamuni Buddha expound the law and failing to grasp the meaning of this gesture, covertly glanced at one another. Only

Mahakasyapa, one of the Ten Brethren, broke into a smile.

Sakyamuni thereupon said: "I have the pure method of Zen and a clear Zen mind and I now bestow them upon Kasyapa!" (*Dafan Tianwang Wenfo Jueyi Sutra*).

It is thus, between the serene holding of the flower and the meeting of minds in the smile, in that poetic moment, that Zen was born and was transmitted from the master to the disciple. This was no mechanical transmission, no word was uttered, just the impact of two minds upon each other. Zen lives and thus transcends form, and the subtlety of Zen transcends language.

At the same time that Sakyamuni transmitted Zen to Kasyapa he also gave him a gold embroidered *kasaya* robe and an alms bowl as the symbols of faith, so that Buddhists subsequently became accustomed to referring to the transmission of the practice of Zen as "*yibo xiangchuan*"—the passage of robe and bowl. Kasyapa was the First Patriarch of the Indian School of Zen that was transmitted generation by generation to Bodhidharma, the 28th Patriarch. Bodhidharma came east from western India bringing Zen Buddhism to China and is known as the First Patriarch of the Chinese School. Six generations later we come to the Sixth Patriarch Hui Neng who founded the characteristically Chinese School of Zen.

Four Zen Precepts

Do not be bound by scripture: This means not adhering rigidly to written texts and emphasises the comprehension of significances that lie beyond language. There is a famous Zen text called "Pointing to the Moon" (*zhi yue lu*), using a finger to indicate the moon, a metaphor for the relationship between truth, the moon, and language, the finger. Once the moon is visible, the finger may be forgotten: there is no need to be bound by the text. This is known as "See the moon and forget the finger, return home and discard the questions."

Outside the sect are other narratives: The transmission of Zen differs from other schools of Buddhism and has its own unique methods. Zen emphasises transmission by "holding the flower and smiling"—from mind to mind and through the impression of mind upon mind. Zen masters have always sought to convey the deepest subtleties of Zen by the analogous symbolisms of the staff, the sudden shout, the raised finger, the clenched fist, the alms bowl and in the wearing of clothes and the act of eating.

Go straight to the heart: All Zen's stimuli, language

and methods are designed to cut through the here and now to the heart of enlightenment that is within all of us. The Zen master's every effort is made to make us return to the source of living, to the pure unpolluted limpid wellspring of life.

Perceive one's own nature and become Buddha: When we can see our heart and our mind, then we have achieved an enlightened Buddha-hood.

To explain these precepts further and more clearly, let us look at some classic Buddhist fables.

The Merchant and His Four Friends

There was once a merchant who had four friends. He obeyed every word of his first friend and gave him the best of everything—clothes, food and housing. His second friend was of impressive appearance and looked magnificent. The merchant had great respect for him and tried by all means to maintain the relationship, gaining great satisfaction by having such a friend whom he flaunted in front of others. The merchant's attitude to his third friend was rather cooler. But because this friend was a master of cuisine he was extremely satisfied with him. It was only the fourth friend about whose very existence he seemed not to care at all.

One day the merchant had some business at a considerable distance and thought that he would take one of his friends with him to avoid the loneliness of the journey. He asked the first friend who replied that he could only share pleasure not suffering and had no obligation to travel so far with him. Much hurt, the merchant asked his second friend, who said that he realised that the merchant had always been good to him but, then, everybody else was always good to him too, so there was no need for him to accompany him. The unhappy merchant then asked his third friend. The third friend said that he could see him on his way a little but only just as far as the door when he would have to turn back to deal with important matters which awaited his attention. The merchant finally asked his fourth friend. Contrary to his expectations the fourth friend said not a word and set out on the journey with him.

The merchant in this Zen story is nobody other than ourself. That distant destination is no other than the land of death. Consequently the purpose of the story is to state clearly that when, one day, we leave this world, what is there, really, that we can take with us?

The first friend is the friend of food and clothing, that is, one's fleshly body. For many of us our lives revolve around our body and the satisfaction of our sensual organs, but in the end our body cannot go with us.

The second friend is the friend of fame and riches, our wealth, money and status. We pursue them to the point of exhaustion, ever fearful that we have not tried hard enough, and then they desert us.

The third friend is those close to us. Wives, colleagues and companions. That we should be together throughout life with these friends is an affinity to be treasured. But they cannot accompany us when we leave the world.

The fourth friend is the friend of the spirit. Our own spirit and senses. What we can take from this world is a pure, clean spirit. It is only this that stays with us in life and death, that never abandons us or leaves our side, yet we forget its very existence.

In this world we treat our physical body, our profit and riches well. We treat our relatives and colleagues well but we should be treating our spirit well.

What is really unfortunate is that many of us spend our lives in the pursuit and company of our first three friends and utterly neglect our fourth, and it is this fourth friend to whom we really need to pay attention—our life's most treasured conscience and our own nature. The wisdom of Zen calls on us to have concern for our spirit, to treat it well, to stop impetuous behavior and to listen for the sound of the true life, thereby making life itself calmer and more settled.

This classic Buddhist fable points out the basic aim of Zen: to clear the mind and see one's original nature and to became a Buddha through a flash of enlightenment. To understand these four friends is to know one's own spirit and see one's own nature.

Knowing Hot and Cold of Oneself

The word "enlightenment" holds the sense of both "mind" and "I," that is to say "my mind," with the meaning of "I feel in my mind," or "I experience in my mind."

Zen places great importance upon the concept of experience. It is this kind of personal experience that the *Platform Sutra* refers to when it says "When one drinks water, one knows of oneself whether it is hot or cold."

When we drink a glass of water, I say that it is hot and you may also say that it is hot. But although we both say that it is "hot," it is, in fact, not the same. In my case the water may have to be at a temperature of 60 degrees Celsius before I will say that it is hot, but you may say that it is hot when it reaches 45 degrees. Thus while both may say that it is hot, it is only oneself that knows the actual temperature.

The heat or the coldness of a glass of water is like this and in the same way the joy and suffering of life is determined by our own spiritual perception.

Salty Has Its Salty Flavor and Tasteless Its Tasteless Flavor

The great Chinese monk Master Hong Yi (1879-1942) had a good friend, the well known educator Xia Mianzun.

One day Mr Xia came to visit Master Hong Yi and saw that he was eating just a small dish of salted vegetables. Unable to restrain himself, Mr Xia asked: "Isn't that too salty?"

Master Hong Yi replied: "Salty has its salty flavor."

Having eaten, Master Hong Yi poured a glass of plain boiled water and drank it.

Mr Xia asked again: "Isn't that too tasteless?"

Master Hong Yi replied with a smile: "Tasteless has its tasteless flavor."

Mr Xia listened and was very touched.

Salty has the flavor of salt and tasteless the flavor of tastelessness so that no matter whether it is salty or tasteless, both can be enjoyed. It is this frame of mind that is possessed by the enlightened.

The Stillness of Zen Calms the Heart

Turbulent water in a glass cannot reflect an object outside. Our mind is the same. If it is always disturbed and unquiet it cannot reflect external objects. So we must seek the help of Zen to calm us down.

Before the installation of running water, drinking water was fetched from the river. After rain it was often muddy so to purify it people dropped alum into the water tub. After a while the impurities sank to the bottom and the water became crystal clear and drinkable. This is the principal of Zen meditation.

When our mind and spirit are disordered and resemble turbid water Zen meditation, like alum, will precipitate the impurities, cleanse our thinking and clarify the spirit. The Confucian classic, The *Great Learning* said: "Know the limits and then achieve stability, once stable then achieve stillness, once still then achieve peace, once peaceful then think and once thoughtful then one may gain."

The Marvellous Effect of Seated Zen

What is the actual result of Zen meditation?

There was a seller of bean curd who supplied a Buddhist monastery with bean curd every day and often saw many monks sitting cross-legged in single-minded concentration in the monastery hall, though he did not know what they were actually doing. One day, unable to contain himself any longer, he asked the abbot:

"Master, your monks sit there all day from morn to night with their eyes closed and without stirring. What are they up to?"

The abbot smiled benignly and said: "Come along, don't hurry home today, just sit here awhile."

The bean curd seller sat for a while in the manner of the monks. Half an hour later he rushed out of the hall in glee, shouting: "Wonderful, wonderful, who would have thought that there was so much good in sitting cross-legged!"

The abbot smiled: "You've made very quick progress. Tell me what you've learned."

The bean curd seller replied: "Normally my mind is a mess, rather like porridge. But sitting there it was absolutely clear and easy to use and I could remember everything. I suddenly remembered that thirty years ago, my neighbor Little Wang owed me two mao five fen for bean curd and still hasn't paid me!"

This is an amusing story but it contains much to think about. If you can meditate for 15 minutes a day and can keep it up for a month you will achieve a very distinct result. If we can only calm our minds, our true nature and wisdom will be manifested and we will reap an immeasurable benefit.

Casting away and Taking up

If we visited a monastery and asked a Zen master for an explanation of Zen, almost all would reply with the phrase:

See through, cast away, be at ease!

This phrase expresses the real marvels of Zen. Only by seeing through can we cast away. Only by casting away can we be at ease in our life.

As we live in the world we need a calm unhurried sense of ease. The frantic person of today first of all needs to see through and then to cast away.

Casting away Your Cup

There was a girl who made an error of judgement that caused her to lose a much-loved boyfriend. She bitterly regretted this decision and unable to accept the fact, lost the will to eat, lost her complexion and withered away so that she was thinner than a flower stalk.

Utterly disheartened she tormented herself but there was no solution to the problem. When she heard that I knew about the wisdom of Zen she came to see me. After listening to her story I took a beautiful cup and said that she shouldn't be down hearted but should appreciate the cup.

The girl was an art student and was captivated by the beauty and unique shape of the cup. At that point I let go of it, it smashed on the floor and she cried out in sympathy.

I pointed to the broken fragments and said: "You obviously felt sympathy for the cup. But no matter how sympathetic you feel the cup has been smashed and cannot be returned to its original state and cannot be retrieved. I hope that from now on you will remember three things:

"Firstly, it is very difficult indeed to make a fine cup. It is the work of a moment, however, to smash it. So, if you have a beautiful cup you must look after it carefully.

"Secondly, if the cup gets smashed, it can't be made whole again. So when, unfortunately, it does get smashed, you need to be level-headed about it.

"Thirdly, if the cup were of reinforced glass it wouldn't smash so you must make yourself into reinforced glass."

The girl listened and left tearfully having shed a very heavy burden.

She now lives happily, her complexion much better than it was, and much more confident in herself.

Casting away the cup is to be able to see through and to accept; taking up the cup is to recognise the reality and accept the burden. Throughout life everybody must learn these two lessons.

* * *

The aim of Zen is to clear the mind and see one's true nature.

Zen is not bound by scripture and there are other narratives outside the sect. Go straight to the heart and perceive one's nature to become a Buddha.

Zen is in the holding of the flower and the smile in return and in the impression of mind upon mind.

The experiencing of Zen is "like drinking water and knowing hot and cold by oneself."

The function of Zen is to reduce pressure, increase stability and open up wisdom. It resembles a piece of alum that precipitates impurities and clarifies the mind.

As we live in this world, we must see through and cast away. We must also recognize the reality and accept the burden. This is the message of Zen.

Chapter II
Everybody Is Rich

We live in a society with a highly developed material civilization. Nevertheless, many people complain that though their income is greater than it used to be, their sense of satisfaction diminishes by the day; that though their living accommodation is more and more splendid, their outlook is narrower and narrower; though their communications are more and more developed their spiritual connections are fewer and fewer. Everybody can ask themselves, in all honesty, am I happy?

In the several thousand years of China's traditional cultural history there have been three solutions to this perplexing problem—Confucianism, Daoism and Buddhism.

The most important Confucian classical texts are the Four Books and Five Classics. The Four Books comprise The *Great Learning,* the *Doctrine of the Mean,* the *Analects* and *Mencius.* This is the order in which they were arranged by the Song dynasty Confucian scholar Zhu Xi. He made the *Great Learning* the first of the Four Books because its first line reads:

> The principle of the great learning is to manifest innate virtue, to extend it to all and to cease only at the extremes of virtue.

This tells us that the lesson that most needs to be learned during life's course, and the most significant kind of life, lies in manifesting one's own radiant virtue. The *Great Learning* tells us that a sense of virtue is something that we all had originally. All we need to do is to develop it, perfect it and extend it to all.

The Daoist philosopher Li Er wrote famously in *Laozi* of the "return to the state of childhood," meaning that we should escape the world of temptation, confusion and noise and return to the truth and simplicity of the original state of childhood perfection. The highest aspiration of the Daoists was to achieve the realm of "returning to simplicity, going back to the truth." Truth and simplicity is the original state of the uncorrupted life.

Zen's concern in life is to "clarify the mind and perceive its nature" and, like the Daoists and Confucians, to return to our original nature.

This is the treasure of self.

Although all of us possess this treasure, we fail to recognise its value and suffer thereby; because what we seek is not happiness itself, but to be happier than others. This is the root of suffering.

In the midst of comparisons with others and of social climbing we have lost sight of our own treasure and have sought fame and profit, wealth, power and sexual desire, creating a deeply unharmonious situation: one of material progress but qualitative decline, of inflated desire but spiritual atrophy.

Thus our highest priority must be to recognise our own treasure and open the door to happiness.

A Treasure That All Possess

There is a Zen saying:

> No balcony is without its moon and no garden without its spring. (*Compendium of Five Lamps*)

Similarly we all have this priceless treasure within us. But if you do not discover it, it exists in name only. Despite its wealth you remain penniless, like the girl possessed of treasure beyond value but who lived in poverty.

The Penniless Girl's Treasure

This is a classic Zen story. The tale is from the *Nirvana Sutra* and is set in ancient India.

There was once a penniless girl in whose family courtyard was buried a wealth of treasure that nobody knew of.

At the time, there was a person of great wisdom and virtue who was aware of the treasure and wished to tell the girl of its existence. Fearing that the girl would not believe him he thought of a means to accomplish his aim.

He said: "Please could you do a job for me, could you do some weeding?"

The girl replied: "I can't do it for you unless you tell me that there is treasure in the house."

The girl wanted to use this as an excuse to refuse the request since she did not know of the buried treasure. Unexpectedly, the wise one readily said: "I know that there is treasure and what's more, I can tell you where it is buried."

The girl replied: "Nobody in the family knows anything about a treasure, how is it that you do?"

The wise one said: "I really do know of it."

The girl replied: "Right, seeing is believing, I want

to see with my own eyes before I do anything."

The girl followed the wise one to the rear courtyard of her house where, sure enough, he dug up the treasure.

She saw the treasure and was delighted in body and soul and developed a feeling of sincere respect for the wise one.

The penniless girl's home originally possessed priceless treasure, but because it lay undiscovered she remained poverty stricken. Once it was dug up she immediately became possessed of great wealth.

The spiritual world of each of us contains such a treasure. It does not require us to seek it by tramping across mountain and river shod in shoes of iron. The sense of Zen tells us that this wealth is by our side, something that we have and that can, above all, make us happy. We only have to recognise our conscience and our true nature to immediately enrich our innermost being.

It Is Difficult to Find the Jewel Hidden in One's Clothing

Everybody has a backyard in which there is treasure. In

everybody's clothing there is a priceless, hidden jewel although we may not recognise it.

If you find it you will be utterly fulfilled. If not, you will drift the streets in frustrated destitution.

What sort of a jewel is it that we have hidden in our clothing?

This is a philosophy of life expounded in the *Lotus Sutra*.

The Jewel within the Clothing

The *Lotus Sutra* recounts how a poor man went to call on a rich relative and was enthusiastically entertained and became so drunk that he fell into a stupor at the table. Unfortunately the relative then received a note calling him away on immediate official business.

Seeing his poor relative utterly incapable through drink, the rich man took a very valuable jewel, hid it in the folds of his relative's clothing and then hurriedly left.

The poor man, drunk as mud, was unaware of what had happened and when awake and sober, seeing that his host was no longer there, took his leave.

Several years later, he was still drifting about

the streets without a penny. He had no idea that his clothing contained a jewel worth a city's ransom.

Later, by chance, he encountered his rich relative who, seeing his tattered clothing, sighed tearfully and said:

"How can you be so pathetic? Your clothing contained a jewel worth a city's ransom and you are still drifting about the streets!"

The poor man listened in complete surprise. His rich relative told him where in the folds of his clothing the jewel had been secreted and he finally found it. Thereafter he no longer drifted about the streets and lead a life of wealth and happiness.

In this Zen story the jewel in the clothing is enlightenment and wisdom, concealed by the tattered clothing of anxiety and vain aspiration, to the point where the riches of our conscience and true nature remain unknown. Thus, dejected and frustrated in spirit and impoverished as ever, we blunder headlong along the path of life.

The rich relative symbolises the Buddha. "Buddha appears in the world through great causes." This great cause is to inspire us to clarify the mind and perceive its nature and so to achieve enlightenment.

Consequently, the ultimate concern of Zen is to guide us towards the discovery of that jewel in the clothing that we all have and towards the recognition of our conscience and our true nature. Once possessed of the directions of the wise and having discovered the jewel in our lives we can cast off poverty and become a person of enlightenment and of wisdom.

Opening the Inexhaustible Treasure

What is our "original mind and true nature"? The Sixth Patriarch, Master Hui Neng said:

> ...Ones' true nature is of itself pure and undefiled, ...one's nature is neither born nor is it destroyed, ...one's nature is of itself complete and sufficient, ...one's nature is unwavering, ...one's nature can create all states of existence. (*Platform Sutra*)

This is our original mind and true nature and our own treasure.

Diamond-like Vision

There was once a young man who called upon a Zen master hoping that he would teach him the value of life.

The Zen master merely told him to sweep the floor, make tea, receive guests and when unoccupied to calm his mind.

Time passed and the disciple asked the master: "Master! When will tell me the value of life?"

The master smiled and made no reply.

Time passed and the disciple grew agitated and again asked: "Master! When are you really going to tell me the value of life?"

The master thereupon took up a stone and handed it to the disciple saying: "Take this stone to the vegetable market and estimate its price. You only have to find out the price, not sell it."

Most people at the market paid no attention to the stone at all. Eventually one person offered five cash for it. For what? To take it home to crush pickled cabbage with.

The disciple brought the stone back and told the master: "Master, someone offered five cash for it."

The master said: "Good, now take it to the

diamond market and see."

The disciple took the stone to the diamond market and then came dashing back wild with joy and told the master: "Someone there said that it was a perfect diamond and somebody offered 50,000!"

The master laughed and said: "This is a stone that one person wanted to use to crush pickled cabbage and another thought to turn into a jewel worth a city's ransom. There was no change in the stone itself, but seen through whatever eyes you use to view it, its value reflects what you saw.

"Every day you pester me asking: what is the value of life? Now, you should understand it. The view seen through the eyes of the vegetable market and the view seen through the eyes of the diamond market are completely different."

The disciple listened and suddenly understood.

All living beings spend their lives in the headlong pursuit of the most valuable objects in life but very few realise that our eyes and our spiritual senses are the most valuable.

If you view yourself through the eyes of crushed

pickled cabbage, your self then becomes the stone for crushing that pickled cabbage. If you view yourself through the eyes of a diamond then your self becomes a jewel worth a city's ransom.

This jewel of great value is not your expensive lifestyle, wealth or position, but your self-possessed, spiritually stable, optimistic and fulfilled state of Zen-like joy. In the minds of those who pursue money there is nothing but money. In the minds of those who seek power there is only power. The minds of those who seek property contain nothing but property. In this limitless and unending pursuit we have become slaves to gold, power and real estate and have lost our own treasure.

Once somebody has lost their treasure, no matter how exalted their position or however great their wealth they are at a desperate point of no return.

Limitless Benefit

Mankind is innately greedy, craving more wealth, a higher position and more excitement. Living today's increasingly materially abundant life, we are more and more tired and more and more depressed.

When we no longer busily seek the external and look

into the depths of our spirit we can re-discover our own treasure. A treasure which "Needs not exhaustion in its gaining, is inexhaustible in its use, the limitless treasure of the creator" (Su Shi, *First Essay of the Red Cliff*).

As we look at what seems a humdrum life this personal treasure can bestow a limitless benefit on us.

Somebody asked the Zen master Yu Yuan: "Who gains from all those who pan for gold?"—Who really finds true gold as everybody struggles all out for riches?

The master said: "Those who pan the sand at the river side trap themselves, there is treasure at home to be regained!" (*Jing De Record of Transmitting the Light of Buddha*)

So in this world we should be a true seeker after gold.

The True Seeker after Gold

There is the story of two Mexicans who were panning for gold on the banks of the Mississippi river. The men separated at a river junction since one believed that more gold was to be found by panning on the Arkansas river whilst the other thought that the opportunities to make a fortune were greater on the Ohio river.

Ten years later, sure enough, the one on the

Ohio river made his fortune by finding a large quantity of gold dust there. He built quays and laid down roads and the place where he had stopped became a large town. Pittsburgh beside the Ohio river is now commercially prosperous and industrially developed and has benefited from its early opening up.

On the face of it the one who followed the Arkansas river was not so fortunate. There was no news of him from the moment that he left his friend. Some said that he was already buried amongst the fish and others that he had returned to Mexico.

55 years later a natural gold nugget weighing 27 kilos caused a sensation in Pittsburgh. A journalist investigated the nugget and said in his report: This, the largest gold nugget in America, was not found in Pittsburgh but was found by a young man in the fishpond behind his house in the state of Arkansas. His grandfather's diary showed that he had thrown the nugget into the fishpond himself.

Subsequently, a magazine published the diary, a passage of which said: Yesterday, I found another very large gold nugget in the river. Should

I go into town and sell it? If I do that then crowds of people will make their way here and the log cabin that I and my wife built with our own hands, the vegetable patch that we dug with the sweat of our brows, the fishpond at the back, the woodpile at the side, the loyal dog, the smell of beef stew, the sparrows, the sky, the trees, the grass and the peace and independence here will no longer exist. I would rather see the splash of water from this gold nugget as it is thrown into the fishpond than watch helplessly as the life that we have made for ourselves here disappears in front of our eyes. Our life here is too tranquil and too beautiful.

The 1860s saw the emergence of millionaires in America and the widespread pursuit of money but this gold-panner threw away the gold he had gained.

However, we can say that amongst all those who panned for gold it was only he who found it.

However much you spent, could you buy a life as tranquil as an idyll or the treasure of family life as happy and fortunate as this?

* * *

"Break open the inexhaustible treasure, bring forth the jewel beyond value. Eschew the material, manifest the original person!" (*Record of the Sayings of Master Yuanwu Keqin*)

This is to open up the inborn treasure within us all and extract the priceless jewel that it contains so that our self can live a life of happiness and fulfilment without relying on external wealth.

This inexhaustible lifelong treasure lies within the depths of the spirit of each of us and in our life as it is.

Chapter III
Why Are You Unhappy?

Plato said: "Those with gold in their hearts have no need to live beneath a golden roof."

Socrates once looked at a street stall in Athens and after some while remarked: "Hmm, so many things that I don't need!" One with an ardent love of the spiritual life is necessarily indifferent to material extravagance.

The British historian Arnold Toynbee said in the *Toynbee-Ikeda Dialogue* of 1976: "The society of mankind today is at its most dangerous period and this is a consequence that it has brought upon itself." Why is this so? It is because mankind has lost its way through excessive selfishness and corruption.

Unfortunately, Toynbee's forecasts are gradually becoming reality in our own lifetime.

If you have not earned enough for a fine house, top brand car and income of millions, and if you are not that much-envied figure, a successful man, it shows that you are no good and have committed the crime of failure to succeed.

Everybody dreams of this so-called success and madly pursues wealth, status and profit thereby losing their own treasure, their own true mind and original nature.

The Snowballing of Desires

Unhappiness is not caused by too few possessions but by the desire for too many.

A consultant mental health doctor of many years standing once said that the most serious and frequent of all the cases that he had met were those of the lifelong pursuit of more and more things. They were careless of the fact that they already had everything. They just wanted even more. People with these psychological symptoms often said: "If only my wants are satisfied, then I will be happy." Once these desires were realized however, they became bored and nourished greater and more novel desires and longings.

Desire is like a snowball, the more it rolls the larger it gets, swelling ceaselessly so that eventually one's spirit exists in a state of perpetual famine.

The Tang dynasty literary figure and thinker Liu Zongyuan wrote a fable called *The Fuban Beetle*. In the fable, there was a kind of small insect that delighted in picking things up. As it crawled it picked up anything that it met and put it on its back. Slowly, the burden grew and grew and crawling became more and more difficult. Despite this it still kept on carrying things on its back. Somebody took pity on it and unloaded its burden. At the point when it was just able to crawl again it started once more to carry the heavy loads that it had done before. In the end, its burden became heavier and heavier and it was crushed to death by the weight on its own back.

Man is the soul of all living things and should logically be much more intelligent than an insect. But is there really any difference between us and the insect in the way that we conduct our lives? Like the insect we shoulder the burdens of fame, profit and power. Should we really always be seeking more? Should we enjoy loading ourselves with this heavy burden, item by item, and come what may, be unwilling to shed it, so that in the end it is we who are crushed by ourselves?

With unquenchable desires and inexhaustible lust the more successful we are, the more anxious and unhappy we become.

Counting Sheep Is No Cure for Insomnia

There was an insomniac who went to see the doctor

in the hope that he could cure his insomnia.

"That's simple," said the doctor. "You're in the wool business and so are familiar with sheep. When you go to bed tonight count sheep, keep counting and you will soon be asleep."

The next day the insomniac rushed round to the clinic in a fury and scowled at the doctor.

The doctor asked in surprise: "What? What I told you didn't work?"

The insomniac replied: "Before I tried your method, I could at least sleep for two or three hours. But last night I couldn't sleep at all. I counted and counted until I had counted thousands upon thousands of sheep and I still couldn't sleep. Then I thought it's useless with sheep. So I thought of shearing sheep and I sheared pile upon pile of fleeces. Then I thought what am I going to do with all this wool? So I started using the wool to make carpets—I'm a carpet salesman by trade. My mind is now stuffed full of over 10,000 wool carpets."

He sighed and went on: "I'm being driven nearly mad. I've got these 10,000 carpets weighing on my mind. What am I supposed to do?"

Similar to the story of the insomniac counting sheep is the tale of the peasant who dug up a very valuable golden statue of an Arhat[1] from a hill.

The moment his friends learned of the discovery they rushed round to congratulate him.

But the peasant was worried. Hitherto, he had earned a living from tilling the soil, enough to feed and clothe himself and to be happy, carefree and at ease. But from the moment of the discovery of the golden Arhat he had neither eaten nor slept well. After a month he had become a bag of bones.

This was because he was afraid that someone would steal his golden statue, but the other major reason was because from morn to night he racked his brains thinking:

"There are eighteen Arhats all told, but I've only dug up one. Where are the other seventeen? If I could find them too, wouldn't that be great?"

This is called "the never satisfied mind is like a snake trying to swallow an elephant"!

Given this amount of greed what happiness can there be to speak of?

---

[1]Arhat (Ch. *Luohan*). One who has achieved spiritual enlightenment (nirvana) and is therefore not reborn. The eighteen Arhats of Chinese Buddhism are considered to be the guardians of the Buddhist faith.

A single desire is a fetter. A tangled multitude of desires is like links of fetters formed into a long chain. This chain tightly binds our hands and feet and binds our heart and mind as well.

Spinning Oneself into a Cocoon

The *Lankavatara Sutra* says: "All vanities and delusions resemble a silkworm as it spins a cocoon. The silken thread of delusion binds both self and others."

The stronger our desires, the longer the thread of anxiety and worry becomes and the harder it binds us. We then lose our spiritual freedom of space and become lifelong prisoners of desire. Binding the self causes suffering to oneself, and binding others brings harm to them and disharmony to society.

The cocoon spun by the thread of desire is the cage of mankind, the most difficult to break out of. We are confined in this cage from birth to death.

Trammelled within this cocoon of desire we lose our freedom and gain nothing in return.

The Monkey and the Fox
There was a hunter who discovered an effective

way of catching monkeys: On the wall, he placed a bamboo tube into one end of which he put a chicken's egg. The monkey, seeing the egg, reached out to take it. Once he had grasped it he was unable to withdraw his hand from the tube.

In fact, the monkey only had to let go of the egg to be easily able to get his hand out. But because of its excessive greed the monkey was unwilling to let go and had to sit meekly awaiting capture.

There is another fable, similar to the one about the capture of the monkey. There was a fox who discovered a vineyard and drooled with anticipation as he looked at the luscious grapes. However, the vineyard was surrounded by a fence and there was no way that the fox could enter.

The fox looked impatiently at the grapes and unable to get in, circled to and fro in agitation.

Finally, the fox steeled his nerves and starved for three days so that, slimmed down, he could slip through a gap in the fence and eat the grapes.

Having eaten his fill, and in great satisfaction, the fox prepared to leave but then discovered to his horror that he had eaten too much and could not get out.

There was nothing to be done but to starve
for yet another three days in order to leave.

A person, once tempted by desire, knows only the
need to grasp at something. Failing to let go when they
should, they fall into the pit of self-destruction.

We all enter the world empty-handed. Life is spent
in frantic acquisition but when the time comes to leave,
we remain empty-handed and can take nothing with
us.

It is said that, on the point of death, Caesar said to
those around him:

"Place my hands outside my coffin so that all
can see that, great as I was, in death my hands were
empty."

Since we are empty-handed anyway, why do we tire
ourselves out?

Seeing Delusion as Reality

The fundamental reason for the snowballing of desires,
the trammels of the cocoon and exhausting activity grows
from the promptings of desire itself. The birth of desire is
caused by the attachment to the external. Seen through the

eyes of Zen, our painful lifelong pursuit of the external is the mist of an illusion without substance. Attachment to an illusory external and the turning of falsity to truth causes the loss of the tranquillity of spiritual joy.

The Thirsty Deer Pursues the Mirage

Sometimes, driving under the fierce summer sun, we see, 200 yards or so ahead of us, something that seems like a shining pool of water. It looks like water but is not. It is a reflection caused by the sun shining on the tarmac road. The experienced driver knows that however much they accelerate they will never reach it.

Amongst the ten most classic metaphors of Mahayana (Great Vehicle) Buddhism is that of the "sun's flame" or mirage. The *Lankavatara Sutra* says:

> For example, a herd of deer, driven by thirst,
> sees the mirage and think it water. Confused and
> enticed they do not know that it is not water.

The mirage described here is the same kind of phenomenon as the pool of water seen on the road under the summer sun. Thirsty deer see it but however much they hurry they never reach it. How can deer, at the limit of thirst, know this? So they rush on, finally driving themselves to death by exhaustion.

The deer in pursuit of a mirage symbolise the whole-hearted pursuit of the obsessive dangers of illusory externals. In the practice of Zen, Zen masters frequently warn their students against this muddy pool. The Tang dynasty Zen master Da An said:

> If you seek happiness, then happiness is already within your inner heart; if you wish to become a Buddha, then a Buddha already resides within you. But if you insist upon wandering afar like the deer pursuing a mirage, when, then, can you come to enlightenment? (*Jing De Record of Transmitting the Light of Buddha*)

The Zen master meant that our original mind and nature were sufficient of themselves and full of joy. Not to know this and to rush hither and thither in pursuit of this and that is to see the false as real.

The Suffering of Wandering Elsewhere

When we see the false as real and nothingness as substance we lose the original "I."

The Monk and the Constable

There is a joke about a constable who was escorting a monk under arrest. Every day the constable always checked that "monk," "bag," "documents" and "I" were all present before taking to the road.

One evening, the monk wormed his way into the confidence of the constable. He thanked him for trouble he had taken in escorting him on the journey and put out the money to entertain him with food and wine.

Flushed with drink the constable carefully unlocked the monk's fetters.

Wine cup succeeded wine cup until the constable was as drunk as mud. The monk and the owner of the inn then carried him to a room to sleep it off.

In the middle of the night the monk shaved the constable's head, exchanged clothes with him and crept away.

The constable woke in the morning, felt for his bag and the documents and rehearsed: "Right. Bag, documents, still here."

Then, suddenly, pale with fright: "But where's the monk got to?"

He looked round the inn several times. Not

half a shadow was to be found.

Worried out of his mind he scratched his head.

Scratching itself meant nothing, but what he scratched was bald!

The constable felt his head and then shouted: "Oh, the monk's still here! But where have 'I' got to?"

Where have "I" got to is one of the greatest concerns of Zen. Zen advocates "Purifying the mind and seeing one's nature." That is, finding one's original mind and true nature; finding the original "I."

Throughout our lives, we must keep honestly asking ourselves: is the me of now the real me? Where has the original me gone?

* * *

Man suffers not on account of having too little, but on account of desiring yet more.

The hope of gaining yet more leads to being confused and controlled by the external. This is "employing the material to metamorphose the self."

If we wish to throw off the control of the external

so that it no longer continues to snowball, no longer grows longer like the links of the chain or grows thicker and thicker like the cocoon, the key is to dampen the fires of desire in one's heart and return to one's original mind and to the original "I." Free of the control of the external and calmly ridding oneself of the external is known as "employing self to metamorphose the material."

In employing self to metamorphose the material we gain happiness and tranquillity.

Chapter IV
Employing Self to
Metamorphose the Material

Everybody has an original mind and true nature, self's own treasure, an inexhaustible source of wealth throughout our lives. The loss of it leads to the pursuit of the external material world. At the same time, this pursuit brings further loss to the original mind and true nature.

The greatest task in the practice of Zen is to "metamorphose" this state of control by the external material world, to one in which that world is steered by us.

"Employing the material to metamorphose self" means that the external material world has changed us and controls the self.

"Employing self to metamorphose the material" means that the self has changed the external material world and now controls it.

The cause of unending suffering in life is that we have a surfeit of desires and have been enslaved by wealth, property, sex and office. We are not masters of our selves but are fettered and controlled by our environment. Thus we must alter "employing the material to metamorphose self" and make it "employing self to metamorphose the material" and become the leading figure in our own lives.

Losing Oneself to Pursue the Material

The *Surangama Sutra* has a passage that says:

> All sentient beings come from a state without beginning, lose self in pursuit of the material, lose their original mind and are changed by the material.

This passage was a favorite quotation used by Zen masters for teaching.

Searching for the Escaped Girl

Once upon a time, when Sakyamuni was meditating in the seated position in a silent forest he heard, at a distance, the laughter of a young man and woman.

A little later he saw a young girl hurrying

across in front of him towards another part of the forest.

Soon after, a young man appeared in pursuit and seeing Sakyamuni urgently asked:

"Have you just seen a girl running past? She's stolen my purse and money."

Sakyamuni asked impassively in return: "Which is more important, to find the escaping girl or to find your original self?"

The young man had obviously never thought about this problem before and was nonplussed.

Sakyamuni again asked: "What is more important, finding the girl or your original self?"

The young man turned over what Sakyamuni had said in his mind, and finally discovered the stupidity of "losing oneself in pursuit of the material."

In fact, the young man of the story is no other than ourself.

We spend our lives in the pursuit of fame and fortune, wine and women, to the detriment and the loss of our own treasure. Ever growing desire makes us slaves to the material.

Pursuing the Material and Losing Oneself

The loss of self before the pursuit of the material is known as "losing self to pursue the material." But at the same time, when, in the process of the pursuit of the material there is further loss to the self, this is known as "pursuing the material and losing self."

The satisfaction of the basic requirements of life is an established principle that cannot be denied. But over-reliance on this principle and boundless desire will cause us to lose our true nature. Although we live a life of unprecedented material wealth we have lost the most valuable treasure of all.

Life Is like a Puppet

Fa Yan, one of the masters of the Linji sect of the Zen school of the Song dynasty told his pupils a story that went:

As a monk, I entered the town yesterday and heard the sound of cymbals and drums, took a closer look. All I could see was a black cloth round a stage. On the stage were a number of wooden dolls. Some were handsome and others ugly. Some were well dressed and others dressed in rags. These

71

dolls could move, speak, sing, laugh and cry. As I was watching with interest, I suddenly saw the black cloth flutter. Getting closer I saw that there was a man behind it whose hands were pulling the puppets' strings and from whose mouth came an imitation of all sorts of different voices.

As I looked I thought, this is really interesting and couldn't help laughing. I asked him: "What is your name, Sir?" He replied: "Master Monk, never mind the name!   How about just watching?" I was speechless. (*Record of the Sayings of Renowned Monks*)

"Never mind the name (*xing* homophone of *xing* 'nature')" means that the original mind and true nature must be realized through experience and cannot be expressed in words.

The puppeteer behind the black cloth signifies that we are not our own masters and that we are manipulated by others. Those who come together in profit when all prospers and disperse when it does not are, like the puppets, never free of this manipulation.

Behind his outward appearance man is helpless in the extreme and, like the puppets, is everywhere controlled by an invisible string: the string that pulls you and tells you that it is money that you must struggle to earn at all costs for life's needs, that it is status and incessant promotion that is required in life, and if you scrape the top of your head as you clamber upwards then that is fame.

As we busy ourselves about these things, we still believe that we are in control of ourselves. The truth is that we are controlled by, and have become sacrifices to, fame and profit.

Employing Self to Metamorphose the Material

After the quotation from the the *Surangama Sutra* "All sentient beings come from a state without beginning, lose self in pursuit of the material, lose their original mind and are changed by the material" there follows the sentence:

If you can metamorphose the material, then you will become an enlightened Buddha!

The essence of Zen is that it should transcend the confused sights and sounds of the external world, and preserve our spiritual tranquillity and independence in the midst of it.

Zhuangzi said: "The gentleman does not fall slave to the material."

A certain degree of material requirement is needed for the sustenance of life. But the excessive pursuit of the material leads to us being enslaved by it and damages the original mind and true nature.

How can we escape from the predicament of "employing the material to metamorphose self"? There is only one route: that is by "employing self to metamorphose the material." This means using the "I," the self, to change the external material world, to escape its slavery and to become its master.

When you employ self to metamorphose the material you can escape from the character of the property slave or the slave to office, and irrespective of the size of your house you can live comfortably, and irrespective of your rank in office you can live at ease.

A Room Filled with Moonlight

An elderly monk at the end of his life, wished to pass his robe and alms bowl to one of his three disciples, all of whom had considerable powers of understanding. This caused the old monk great difficulty in choosing between them. One bright moonlit night the monk felt that he was about to leave the world and that the time had come to choose a successor.

He called the three disciples to him and gave each a copper cash and sent them to buy something that was both cheap and would fill a room in the monastery. The first and second disciples took the money and left. The third and youngest disciple remained solemnly meditating in the lotus position.

After a while, the eldest disciple returned and told the master that he had used the money to buy several cartloads of straw that would fill a room in the monastery.

The old monk listened and shook his head.

The second disciple returned, took a candle from his sleeve and lit it.

The old monk displayed an expression of satisfaction and at the same time turned his gaze towards the youngest monk at his side who rose slowly to his feet and returned the money he had been given, crossed his arms in obeisance and said:

"Master, what I bought is about to arrive!" As he spoke, he puffed out the candle and the room was plunged into darkness.

The disciple pointed through the door and said: "Look, Master, what your disciple bought has arrived!"

They all looked out and saw the full moon hanging hugely in the sky.

The moonlight flooded into the room, filling it with a crystal radiance.

The old monk was speechless with amazement and wept tears of joy. He took off his kasaya and gently draped it over his disciple's shoulders.

So it is that moving from "employing the material to metamorphose self" to "employing self to metamorphose the material" is so simple. We merely have to grasp the scale of it, open our mind and spirit and the fresh air of contentment and the beautiful moonlight will come flooding in. Moreover, this gift of nature can be bought for nothing. So, in fact, we can relax a little in our lives.

As long as your mind is at ease and full of joy there will always be bright moonlight and a home or yurt wherever you go. The key to transformation lies in a single thought.

Be at Ease and in Command

In losing self to pursue the material and in pursuing the material and losing self, man is like a puppet tightly controlled by external forces, or a spinning top fiercely lashed by the whip of desire. It is only by "employing self to metamorphose the material" that we can become our own master and escape the slavery of property, sex and wealth.

We must keep reminding ourselves to be our own master!

The Master

The Zen master Shi Yan seated on a stone in meditation, often conversed with himself.

"Master!" he called to self.

"Uh!" self replied.

"Wake up, from now on, don't be deceived by others!"

"Of course not, of course not!" (*Compendium of Five Lamps*)

The "Master" that Shi Yan called to is our life's true self, our original mind and true nature. We must warn our self not to be changed by the external material and not to become a puppet or a spinning top.

When you become your own master, you can freely arrange your own time and life.

* * *

The loss of original mind and true nature leads to the pursuit of the external material world, and the pursuit of the external material world of itself causes further loss to the original mind and true nature.

Consequently, in order to avoid being changed by the material, this situation has to be reversed so that self transforms the external material world and comes to control it instead.

At this point, we are no longer puppets or spinning tops and have overcome the attraction of the external material world. With a heroic and unwavering mind we can smile calmly at the swirling dust of the limitless worlds.

The concrete way of "employing self to metamorphose the material" is that sharp edged weapon of Zen—"the gateway beyond all others."

Chapter V
The Ultimate Gateway
that Transcends All

The Song dynasty Zen master Yuanwu Keqin said: "Spring has neither high nor low but flower stems are both long and short." (*Record of the Sayings of Master Yuanwu Keqin*)

This Zen saying is a vivid description of mankind's sense of difference that generally prefers the luxuriant flower with its heady perfume to simple flowers with little scent.

In fact, whether "long" or "short," all flowers are a manifestation of nature and there is no need for mankind to view them in terms of length. However, because of this sense of difference man has created the concept of like and dislike, has obscured the eyes of wisdom, dimmed the clarity of the natural universe and the true face of man and society, and has lost self amidst the distinctions drawn between beauty and ugliness.

Because of the existence of opposites mankind has

created any number of obsessive delusions and vexations. If we wish to root out vexation we must transcend the world of opposites. To do this we have to rid ourselves of that deep-rooted sense of differences that lies in our consciousness. This is a very practical benefit that the wisdom of Zen can give to life.

The "ultimate gateway" is the basic and best means of disposing with attachment, purifying the mind and seeing one's nature. Through it we can transcend all opposites and nurture a relaxed, calm state of mind.

The ultimate gateway makes a complete, unified whole from the relativist concepts of like and dislike, rich and poor, noble and base, senior and junior, and large and small, so that we can reach a wise, perfect, understanding of the problems of self and other, praise and blame, adversity and success, and life and death.

No Distinction Exists between Self and Other

No distinction between self and other means that they are indivisible. You (other) and I (self) were originally two distinct life forms. Why should they be indivisible? It is because all matter exists in a mutual relationship, and is born, develops and dies from definite conditions and mutual functions. It lacks a fixed immutable and independent nature.

All matter is produced from the fusion of many causes and disappears and dies through the break up and dispersal of them. Consequently, self and other are mutually interdependent and interactive, and lack any essential distinction.

When "I" looks at a landscape of hills and rivers and at all living things, "I" exists within them all and they all exist within "I."

Chiyo and the Morning Glory

There is a beautiful haiku by the 16th century Japanese poet Tachibana Ginchiyo:

> Oh! morning glory!
> Entwines the pail,
> I must fetch water.

Early on a June morning when Chiyo went out to draw water, she found to her surprise that the water bucket beside the well was entwined by a flowering morning glory. Breathless and trembling at its tender beauty she was so deeply moved by the scene that even after thought she could not find the words to describe it and merely said:

Oh, morning glory!

Short as it is, this phrase is full of meaning and demonstrates the poet's complete intoxication with the beauty of a sight that contained "a truth within that defies words."

Chiyo, the poet was so utterly entranced by the beauty of the morning glory that it was some time before she recovered from her daze.

When we look at the blossoming of a flower with the attentive gaze of the spirit of Zen we can feel great beauty. In that moment, like Chiyo, we are wholly and totally immersed in that beauty. "I" becomes the morning glory and the morning glory becomes "I" and there is no boundary between self and other.

Pause Awhile from Slander and Renown

In Zen there are eight causes, divided into four pairs, that produce a strong emotional reaction. They are: advantage and disadvantage; defamation and reputation; praise and mockery; suffering and joy.

Anything that conforms to one's aspirations is termed an advantage, anything that does not is a disadvantage.

Slander behind one's back is termed defamation but secret praise is called reputation.

Open praise is called praise but open ridicule is called mockery.

Vexation of mind and body is called suffering but happiness of mind and body is called joy.

Because these eight causes can fan and inflame the emotions they are known as the "Eight Winds."

There is a Zen saying: "The Eight Winds cannot blow away the moon at the margin of heaven" meaning that one skilled in the art of cultivation, whose nature is like that of the moon, remains as immoveable as a mountain however hard the Eight Winds may blow. To be unmoved by the Eight Winds is an advanced Buddhist practice. But to really achieve it is extremely difficult.

Su Dongpo and Fo Yin

When the Song dynasty literary figure Su Dongpo occupied a post at Guazhou on the northern bank of the Yangtse river he became friendly with the Zen master Fo Yin, abbot of the Jin Shan monastery on the opposite bank. Su Dongpo, considered one of the two or three most learned of the literati, was fond of discussing Daoism and Zen and his poetry often displayed elements of Zen. One particular day, feeling that he had gained something from Zen meditation, he wrote a Zen poem full of self-satisfaction and sent it across the river to the abbot with a servant, instructing the servant to ask the abbot for his comments and to bring back the abbot's reply. The poem read:

> Obeisance to the heaven of heavens,
> my wisdom illuminates the worlds.
> Unmoved by the Eight Winds, I sit
> upon the purple lotus throne!

Outwardly, this poem appears to praise Buddhism. In fact it applauds the writer's own determination and ability. When the Zen master Fo Yin read the poem he shook his head, smiled, took up his brush and wrote on it the single word "fart."

Not long after, the servant returned and reported that he had delivered the verse and that the abbot had looked at it and then written "fart" in the margin and thrown it on the floor. He had quickly picked it up and brought it back.

Su Dongpo listened and in a fury prepared a boat intending to cross the river and have it out with the abbot himself.

Long before the boat reached the monastery, the Zen master Fo Yin could be seen waiting on the river bank. As soon as Su Dongpo saw Fo Yin he said furiously: "Master Monk, we're old friends, it doesn't matter if you don't praise my poem, but why do you have to use such offensive language?"

Fo Yin said unconcernedly: "What offensive language?"

Su Dongpo thereupon pointed out the word in the margin to Fo Yin.

Fo Yin smiled and said: "Is the learned graduate so really 'unmoved by the Eight Winds'?"

Su Dongpo responded: "Naturally, naturally, that goes without saying!"

Fo Yin laughed and said: "Fine! Fine! Unmoved by the Eight Winds then, but blown across the river by a fart!"

Su Dongpo burst out laughing and said: "I really have fallen into your hands today!"

In the real world there are too many of these various "winds" and we spin amongst them every day. The winds of fame, profit, money, sex and nepotism all blow constantly. Are we really in any position to "sit upon the purple lotus throne"?

Taking Neither Success Nor Adversity to Heart

In life there are times of adversity and of success. There is the weather of peace and prosperity and days of wind and rain. There is the high tide of triumph and the troughs of despair. If we can deal with all this in a state of wisdom we can be stable, relaxed and at ease.

Home Is the Place for Calmness of Heart

In his last years, after a storm-tossed political life, Su Dongpo returned to the capital from distant parts to a post in the Hanlin Academy. A little later his friend Wang Dingguo was recalled from the south. The two became close drinking companions. At a banquet Wang Dingguo made his singing girl, Rounu, induce Su Dongpo to drink wine. Rounu had delicate features and winning ways, but what most attracted Su Dongpo was her calm, even temperament. He asked her: "Your family lives in the capital, but you followed your master in the south for all those years. The conditions there are terrible. Didn't you suffer?"

Rounu replied: "Home is the place for calmness of heart."

Su Dongpo was stunned that such a delicate and charming girl should have such an unaffected, transcendental mind.

This kind of attitude was also of great help to Su Dongpo himself during his chequered career. He, too, had the breadth of mind that supported the idea of "home is the place for calmness of heart" and when demoted and exiled to the wilds of the south remained completely optimistic.

It is no use blaming the world, but it is in being grateful for small mercies and accepting the suffering that others find difficult that we can discover the joy and comfort of life.

If you are attached to a life of elaborate sophistication, then suffering will increase when times are bleak. But if you are relaxed and detached amidst the elaborate life there can be no suffering in disappointment. This is what is meant in the *Vegetable Root Discourse* of Hong Zicheng when it says: "Be alarmed by neither favor nor disgrace, watch the flowers in the courtyard as they blossom and fade; come and go without aspiration, follow the clouds freely as they billow and disperse." It is also what Su Dongpo himself said: "In happy stability one can take joy in defeat."

This is the ultimate gateway to being able to transcend both success and adversity, loss and gain, victory and defeat.

Life and Death Are Natural

Transcending life and death by means of the ultimate gateway is like ice and water or lifting up and putting down your foot.

Water freezes at low temperatures and becomes ice; ice melts at high temperatures and becomes water. Although both are different in form there is no difference at all in their nature.

In the act of walking we are walking when we lift our foot up and when we put it down.

If we regard life and death with this same mental attitude, then as Tagore's prose poem said:

Life is like the lustre of flowers in spring and death like the quiet beauty of leaves in autumn.

If we look on death with this ordinary point of view then it becomes a "return" and not a road to be feared.

We should know that living and dying, like the opening of flowers and the falling of leaves, is a completely natural phenomenon.

We Are All Passing Travellers

Master Han Shan was one of the four great masters of the late Ming dynasty. Once, while travelling, he lost his way and after walking for some time through a night as black as lacquer he at last saw a light. Focussing his eyes he saw that it was a family home. Master Han Shan was delighted and quickly knocked on the door and asked for lodging for the night.

The householder heard his request and with an expressionless face refused, saying: "Sorry, please find somewhere else. My house is not an inn!"

The master smiled and said: "You have it wrong, your house is indeed an inn! I just need you to answer three questions honestly and I can prove that your house is an inn."

The householder said: "I don't believe you! But if you can persuade me, I'll let you in."

The master then asked: "Who lived here before you?"

The householder replied: "My father!"

"Then, who was the householder before your esteemed father?"

"My grandfather!"

"And if you, young master, pass on, who will become the householder then?"

"My son!"

Master Han Shan laughed and said: "There you are, you see! You are only living here temporarily, and everybody is a traveller like me."

The householder reckoned that he made sense and asked him in.

Master Han Shan spent a comfortable night there.

* * *

"The gate beyond all others" is Zen's powerful weapon for transcending the relativism of opposites and achieving psychological well-being.

Transcending the relativism of self and others is like

appreciating flowers but not picking them and embracing others with a thankful heart; it is the same world with the same dream.

Once the opposites of praise and slander have been transcended, one becomes like the moon unmoved by the Eight Winds and no longer wandering aimlessly.

Once the opposites of success and defeat have been transcended one has mastered the concept of non-involvement, and gain and loss are of no concern. There can be happiness in success but joy in defeat as well.

Once the relative opposites of misfortune and *bodhi* (enlightenment) are transcended it becomes like walking along a riverbank without getting your feet wet, or passing through undergrowth without leaves sticking to you.

Once the opposites of life and death are transcended all is unruffled serenity, so that life is like the lustre of flowers in spring and death the tints of autumn.

To transcend all opposites is to "Escape confused delusion and achieve Nirvana." (*Heart Sutra*)

The world of Nirvana is one of the dissolution and scattering of the relative opposites of vain delusion, of differences and attachment: a world of a life of light winds and cloudless clear sky, a world that transcends trouble and life and death.

Chapter VI
That Which Has Form Is Void and That Which Is Void Has Form

This phrase is the most popular of modern Zen colloquialisms. It comes from one of the classics of Zen, the *Heart Sutra*. Its full title is the *Prajna Paramita Heart Sutra*, prajna meaning "wisdom" and paramita meaning "to reach the other side." "Prajna paramita" means that the wisdom of Zen is like a boat that will carry us from the shores of life's troubles and of death to the far shore of happiness and freedom.

The 260 character the *Heart Sutra* contains the principles and essence of the 600-volume *Mahaprajna Paramita Sutra*, and is mainly a description of the fundamental principles of the void.

The *Heart Sutra* says:

That which has form is void and that which is void has form. So it is with feeling, thought, action and knowledge.

"Form" indicates material phenomena; feeling, thought, action and knowledge are mental phenomena.

This quotation explains that in this context "void" describes the nature of void and not the state of "emptiness" in which nothing exists.

Why is everything void? It is because all matter arises from a combination of causes, hence it is void in nature. This is called void by original nature. On the other hand, it is precisely because of this that when various kinds of cause are combined matter may be produced.

The Consideration of Form as Void

The four elements of the human body are the four characteristics of "Earth, Wind, Fire and Water." Considered from the angle of "form is void" all are void.

Earth refers to its solid characteristics. The body is supported by the skeleton, the solid characteristic of the earth element.

Fire refers to the characteristic of warmth. Body temperature is the warm characteristic of the fire element.

Wind refers to the characteristic of flow. Breath is the

flow characteristic of the wind element.

Water is the characteristic of wetness. Blood, tears and saliva are the wet characteristics of the water element.

Because the body is formed from a combination of elements it is void by nature, but must also exist in a state of harmony. If there is no harmony there is trouble.

Illness is called "disharmony of the elements" and death the "scattering of the four elements."

From the Zen point of view, not only are the four elements void, but everything in the world of man also exists in a state of impermanence and change:

Physiological impermanence is represented by birth, age, illness and death;

Mental impermanence is represented by cause, existence, change and extinction;

Physical impermanence is represented by creation, existence, decay and void.

The importance of the *Mahaprajna Paramita Sutra* can be gauged by the fact that the great teacher of Buddhism, Sakyamuni, spent 22 years of his life expounding its 600 volumes. The *Heart Sutra* shares its basic outline and can be summarised as:

> All phenomena are without substance and in
> the end void and unreal!

As Splendid as Sand

This is an astonishing story of Zen process art.

In February 2001, in a New York art gallery, two Zen masters created a picture to demonstrate Zen art. The picture (a Medicine Buddha mandala) was created from colored sand and took nearly a month to create, working many hours a day to produce an image of the world of Zen and of all sentient beings.

The work was rigorously constructed and brightly colored and the sand gave it a sense of hierarchy to produce a representation of a perfect and extensive world. As the creation of the picture proceeded, the number of spectators increased and the mandala itself become more and more delicate.

Finally, what appeared before the eyes of the beholder was the ultimate in splendor.

The luxuriant detail of the artists' work astonished the sight and spirit of the onlookers but, while they were immersed in and applauding the brilliance of the picture, the two Zen masters, in a sudden and unexpected act, produced brushes and swept away the whole painstakingly constructed mandala.

The lifelike figures, the thriving lives, the imposing temples, the elaborate detail became fine sand trickling slowly through the hands of the monks, to be carried to a stream and tipped away where it dissolved and disappeared, never to return.

In a poignant gesture the two Zen masters had returned that splendid world to the void, an act that enlightens us all.

In the beginning, behind all that brilliance, there was just a handful of sand.

No matter how imposing your appearance, how vigorous your age, how shining your reputation, how blazing your power, or how overwhelming your wealth, in the end, even greater splendor would just be a handful of sand.

Nevertheless, as you face the splendor of that picture created from sand, are you as attached and deluded as you were?

In this mortal realm of dust, nobody is willing to absent themselves from the splendors of the physical world. However, we must recognize clearly that in our short life nothing we have created or experienced is anything but a handful of fine sand. Once we perceive this we can then calmly cast it away.

See through and Cast away

In boundless space, rivers, hills and land are the merest specks of dust, like grains in the ocean; let alone mankind within that speck, so pitifully and infinitesimally minute!

In time without beginning and end, man's corporeal body is like a soap bubble, a transient spark; let alone any achievement outside the bubble, vanished like smoke in a flash.

Unless we achieve enlightenment, how are we to possess a mind that can see through and cast away?

How can we see through? If we wait until the splendor has turned to a handful of sand it will be too late. But if we can see through when that splendor is at its greatest, that is called: "all things corporeal are void in essence."

All Things Corporeal Are Void in Essence

Li Jing, the second emperor of the southern Tang regime of the period of the Five Dynasties and Ten States once invited the Zen master Fa Yan to join him in appreciating some flowering peonies. Fa Yan thereupon wrote a poem:

Lustrous in the morning dew, fragrant

in the evening breeze.
Why wait for the blooms to droop,
to know the empty void?

The first line describes an ordinary person's impression as he looks at the flowers but the second is the perception of the Zen master Fa Yan as he gazed at the peonies. At the very moment that they are at their most lustrous, we must be clearly aware of their true nature and that their fate is void.

To comprehend that all things corporeal are void in essence is to avoid being caught up with the world, being seduced by the external environment or being deceived by appearances.

The Consideration of Void as Form

It is easy for people to become attached to the external appearance of delusion and to "form" and thus, with insatiable greed and ignorant of impermanence, to be drawn towards pragmatism. To eradicate this ill Zen proclaims that "form is void" and that people should not

become attached to external appearances. Once attached
to external appearance, even the mental effort of a lifetime
will be as void and empty as drawing water in a bamboo
basket.

However, there are those who on learning that "form
is void" become attached to the void, believing that if
they are to transcend suffering and achieve liberation they
must distance themselves from "form" thereby becoming
attached to "void" itself. To become attached to "void"
and not to know responsibility is to be drawn into nihilism.
Once attached, the void becomes dead ash, stagnant water,
an empty nothingness of annihilation.

Consequently Zen also says "void is form" and
calls on those who wallow in this nothingness of
annihilation to emerge and assume responsibilities and
obligations.

Grasping the Void

The Zen master Shi Gong enquired of Zen master
Xi Tang: "How can you get a grip of the empty
void?"

Xi Tang made a snatching gesture in the air.

Shi Gong said: "If you do it that way, you
really won't be able to grasp the void."

Xi Tang asked: "Then, how would you

actually do it?"

Shi Gong forcefully twisted Xi Tang's nose and Xi Tang cried out in pain.

Shi Gong said: "That's the only way to grip the void!"

(*Compendium of Five Lamps*)

In this *koan*[1] , when Xi Tang gestured in the air it was to regard "void" as nothing, thereby falling into a pool of stagnant water. Zen says "Dead water holds no dragons." No intelligent life exists in stagnant water. This sort of void is called "utter emptiness," the void of stupidity, the void of annihilation, the empty void of mortal extinction. In Zen, this is the void which is most opposed and most to be avoided.

Shi Gong tweaked Xi Tong's nose in order to correct his misunderstanding. There are two layers of meaning here: one was to alter the erroneous direction of his misunderstanding, the other was to cause him to feel pain and to feel that although "form" is void, "void" is also "form" and that this "void" is not empty but contains "form"—the existence of a nose.

---

[1] A rhetorical device designed to stimulate enlightenment.

To Take up Conscientiously

Only by seeing through can we put down.

Only by recognizing accurately can we take up.

Void is form, "form" is all that we see around us everyday, its original nature is void but we cannot just throw it away because of this. In Zen, the void that is not a void, the void that is not empty, is the only "true void" and is the highest level of void. If we recognize this clearly we can experience the spirit of the true void and take up responsibility and assume obligation.

Putting down is not the same as abandoning. Abandoning is absolute, putting down is relative. Putting down is the better to take up.

Abandoning everything leaves a carcase. This kind of person becomes a walking corpse.

The Sunbathing Carcase

There was a lonely youth leaning against a tree sunbathing. He was ragged and depressed, yawning dispiritedly.

A Zen master came by and asked: "Young man, the weather's so good, why aren't you working instead of standing sighing here?"

The youth sighed and said: "I've got nothing

in the world except this carcase of mine. Why should I take the trouble to go to work? All I do every day is to bathe this carcase of mine in the sun."

"Have you no family?"

"No. Raising a family is too much trouble, just as well not to."

'Isn't there anybody that you like?"

"No. Hate follows love and breaking up follows coming together, just as well not to fall in love."

"Have you no friends?"

"No. Rather than lose them later, it's just as well not to make friends in the first place."

"Don't you want to work?"

"No. You only work to make money. However much you make, you only end up empty-handed. This being the case, why bother to expend all that energy?"

The master gave him a length of cord saying: "Since that's the case, take this length of cord."

The young man was puzzled and said: "What would I do with this length of cord?"

The Zen master said: "Off you go and hang yourself. According to what you say, there's life and then death. Rather than being unable to avoid death in the end it's just as well not to live now. I want to help you succeed, so that you can hang yourself at once."

Many of those who study Zen mistakenly believe that having studied and "seen through the red dust," there is no more to be done. This is a great error and utterly absurd.

Zen holds that "Enlightening life, dedicating life" is life's ideal.

"Enlightening life" is "form is void." That is, to put down. "Consecrating life" is "void is form." That is, to take up.

* * *

To fully grasp the concept of "form is void and void is form" is to penetrate the depths of Zen concentration (*samadhi*): form arises from a combination of causes, its original nature is void; it is precisely because the original nature of form is void that the combination of various causes gives rise to matter.

The world does not possess absolute form, nor does it possess absolute void so one should not be prejudiced towards the one or the other. Attachment to "form" leads to hedonism and attachment to "void" to nihilism.

To rid oneself of the state of attachment to the material one has to comprehend that "form is void"; to eliminate the concept of the nothingness of material one has to comprehend that "void is form."

To comprehend that "form is void" is to be brave enough to "put down"; to comprehend that "void is form" is to be brave enough to "take up."

What is put down is attachment and what is taken up is responsibility.

"Form is void" is an enlightened life. "Void is form" is a dedicated life.

Chapter VII
Create the Will Not to Dwell in Temptation

The greatest Zen master in Chinese history was the Sixth Patriarch, Hui Neng. His speech and behavior while preaching Zen was noted down by his disciples and formed the *Platform Sutra*, the only one of the Chinese writings on Zen to be termed a "Sutra."

Hui Neng was born into poverty and as a young man supported his family by selling firewood. One day, at a market, he heard a customer chanting the phrase:

Create the will not to dwell in temptation.

Hui Neng was fascinated by this phrase and asked the customer which sutra it was and where it came from. The customer replied that it was from the *Diamond Sutra*, a major Buddhist classic, and that it came from the Dongshan Zen temple in the east of Huangmei county where Master Hong Ren was preaching. As soon as he heard it, Hui Neng made up his mind, settled his mother and set out to study Zen at the Dong Shan temple.

One evening, after Hui Neng had been studying under Master Hong Ren, he was listening to him expound the *Diamond Sutra*. When he reached the phrase "create the will not to dwell in temptation," Hui Neng suddenly attained a moment of enlightenment, succeeded to the robe and alms bowl of Hong Ren and became the Sixth Patriarch.

"Create the will not to dwell in temptation" is the most famous line in the *Diamond Sutra*. It contains a subtle connection between "not dwelling" (in temptation) and "creating the will." "Not dwelling in temptation" refers to not clinging to an attachment to anything material, or being emotionally attached to it, so that no obstacle stands in the way of achieving freedom without care.

Nevertheless "not dwelling" does not mean a total unawareness or lack of reaction to the external material world. Were it so, it would mean a total emptiness like a dead tree. Consequently at the same time as "not dwelling" there must be "the creation of the will," a will or mind as clear as still water that mirrors the universe. When things happen, they can be dealt with naturally. When they have passed the situation returns to its original tranquillity.

In the swirling red dust of today's life, creating the will

not to dwell in temptation is extremely difficult to attain.

To understand the core of this concept is to grasp the essence of all Zen.

The Zen Mind Does Not Dwell

In the world of red dust we are faced by the temptations of money, sex, power and position. If, faced with these multitudinous temptations, we can overcome and transcend them, that is "not dwelling in temptation." Very many people busily spend their lives dwelling upon sex when they see it, dwelling on fame when they see it and dwelling on money. Consequently they exhaust themselves to the point of no return, both physically and mentally.

Keeping An Eye on the Six Dusts

Eyes, ears, nose, tongue, body and thought are known as the "six roots," root meaning something that can grow. Plants have roots that can grow into a stalk; man has six roots which can develop into the six corresponding senses of sight, hearing, smell, taste, touch and thought.

In the same way that the six roots give rise to the six senses, the six senses relate to six kinds of material objects and act as a medium between the two. The eye sees form, the ear hears sound, the nose smells fragrance, the body contacts (contact being the touching of a material object), and thought embraces the imagining of things. This makes up the six entities of form, sound, fragrance, taste, touch and imagination.

In Zen, these are known as the "six dusts" since like dust they can pollute man's original mind and true nature.

Laozi warned of this danger in the *Classic of Morality* (*Dao De Jing*) when he said:

> The five forms blind the eyes, the five sounds
> deafen the ears, the five tastes damage the palate,
> hunting maddens the heart and the acquisition of
> rare goods damages behavior.

Everybody likes to listen to beautiful sounds and to see beautiful things; these are external invaders. Everybody has easily aroused emotions and desires incapable of satisfaction; these psychological evils are the enemy within that is most to be feared.

So long as self, the master of one's body, maintains vigilance, these internal enemies and external invaders can become aids to the cultivation of morality.

Those who practise Zen resemble guards who protect

a castle moat, standing sentry by night and day, ever vigilant, ever on guard against the hidden attacks of the enemy. When the eye sees form but is not captivated, when the ear hears sound but is not seduced, when the nose smells fragrance but is not confused, then that is control of the "six dusts."

"Not dwelling" is not allowing the mind to dwell on the "six dusts." It is only by not doing so that we can finally achieve freedom and ease of mind.

Not Dwelling and Creating the Will

The Zen mind should "not dwell," but a one-sided emphasis on "not dwelling" risks falling into the stagnant waters of annihilation, thereby losing life's vitality and setting out on the road towards mere passive disengagement.

Consequently, at the same time as "not dwelling" there must be "the creation of the will." When these are combined it becomes "not dwelling and creating the will" which prevents attachment to external things and the loss of self in the swirling red dust, whilst at the same time providing a mirror that reflects external things and is full of vitality.

The Wind in the Bamboos and the
Geese over the Water

There is a well-known saying of the Zen master Yi Huai which once caused a considerable stir amongst the temples of Zen Buddhism:

> If a goose flies across the sky its shadow is reflected in the water. When there is no trace of the goose, the water no longer retains its shadow.
> (*Forest Record*)

The water is our spirit and the goose represents external material things.

When events occur our mind produces a natural response; after the event our mind returns to its original tranquillity.

This is the essence of "not dwelling and creating the will."

The Ming dynasty author Hong Zicheng used this idea in his *Vegetable Root Discourse* when he wrote:

> The wind blows through the bamboos but leaves no sound behind; the goose flies over the pool but leaves no shadow. So it is that the mind of a gentleman reacts to events as they occur but

returns to the void afterwards.

"Wind" and "goose" are external material objects; the bamboo grove and the pool are our minds. There has to be a natural reaction to all things and at the same time the maintenance of clarity of mind and of tranquillity. Like the bamboo grove as it returns to stillness after the wind has passed, and like the pool that maintains its original unruffled clarity after the goose has flown, in life this alone is the realm of enlightenment.

Master Fo Yin said: "All day long we are entangled in the mundane but all day long we are free beyond the material." This sentence stays in the memory.

Put Body and Arrow Out of Mind

Not dwelling and creating the will can develop the potential of the mind to its uttermost. In archery it becomes a weapon through which martial arts experts can realise their potential and victoriously overcome the enemy.

Realising Zen through the Study of Archery
The Zen master Nan Quan once asked the Zen master Shen Shan: "What are you doing?"

Shen Shan replied: "Beating a gong."

Nan Quan said: "Are you using your hand or your foot?"

Shen Shan replied puzzled: "I don't understand, please tell me whether you can see I'm using my hand or my foot or not."

Nan Quan told him: "Remember this well. There will be an opportunity in the future to ask somebody with clarity of vision."

Subsequently another Zen master who had heard this exchange said: "Only those with neither hands nor feet can really beat a gong!"

(*Jing De Record of Transmitting the Light of Buddha*)

How is it that only those without hands or feet can "really" beat a gong?

The master meant that under normal circumstances we are aware of whether we are using our hand or another part of our body to perform an action and that this awareness is a distraction which influences our reactions and prevents us from putting our whole heart into the action and achieving the highest standards.

But when there is neither "hand" nor "foot" and in a state where the existence of both hands and feet has been forgotten, we do not think anymore of whether we are using hand or foot. We are no longer an observer of our own behavior and actions. At this point, there is nothing beyond the existence of the aim and the means of achieving it, so that the whole body and mind can be concentrated upon realising its greatest potential.

This is "not dwelling and creating the will" in ordinary life.

In the 1920s, the German philosopher Eugen Herrigel visited Japan to find a Zen master with whom to study meditation. He subsequently wrote a book, *Zen in the Art of Archery* in which he vividly described the state of "not dwelling and creating the will." In the book, he recounted how he had spent many years with a master in the study of archery and that he had finally learned how, by "using strength without effort," drawing the bow "spiritually," and releasing the string "without a target," he had enabled the arrow to leave his bow hand of its own volition "as ripe fruit drops from the tree."

Once he had reached perfection it was if the bow, arrow, target and bow hand had all merged into one. At this point he felt that it was not he himself who was the archer but that it was this other "one" that had performed the action for him.

At this stage, not only was "not dwelling" incorporated

in forgetting the subjective "I" and the objective arrow and target, but "creating the will" was also involved in using a mind that was without mind to cause the arrow to leave his bow hand "as ripe fruit drops from the tree."

Not a Leaf Sticks

In the swirling red dust, using "not dwelling and creating the will" when faced with the absorbing attractions of sex can bring similar ease of mind.

Carrying the Girl across the Stream

The Zen master Tan Shan normally enjoined his disciples and students of Zen to observe discipline and keep away from feminine charms. His disciples regarded this warning as a rule never to be broken.

Tan Shan once took one of his young disciples on a walk.

It poured with rain and the ground became like a river. A young girl stood hesitantly at the edge of the water, looking from side to side, uncertain of how to cross without getting her skirt wet.

Master Tan Shan saw the situation, held out his arms and said expansively: "Come along, young lady," picked her up and carried her across to the other side. The girl glanced back with a smile, gave her thanks and went on her way.

Master Tan Shan walked on as if nothing had happened. But that backward glance and smile had sent the disciple's heart galloping and his pulse racing.

After several miles, the young disciple could no longer hold back and burst out: "Master, aren't you always telling us that those who leave home to become monks should beware of feminine charm? The girl we met today was absolutely beautiful. Why did you have to pick her up and carry her across?"

Master Tan Shan laughed and said: "Oh, you mean that girl? I put her down long ago, but you still carry her in your heart!"

To pick up a girl from a muddy road and carry her across a stream is to help someone overcome a difficulty. There is no impurity of heart: it is an act of compassion. There may be attraction in the eye but not in the heart. The disciple, however, believing that his master had seized the opportunity to get close to a woman and that he should not have done so, carried on walking for several miles thinking about it. There may have been no attraction in his eye but there was attraction in his heart. There was all the difference in the world between the situation of the master and that of his pupil.

In this story, the Zen master occupied the realm of "not dwelling and creating the will." The will he created was that of wisdom and compassion. His disciple occupied the realm of "dwelling" and the will or mind he created was one of difference and vexation.

Creating the will without dwelling means that you carry or take up when you should without hesitation, and put down when you should put down, avoiding being embroiled in the mud. There should be no impurity of mind in taking up and no strings attached when you put down.

It is only the mind of "not dwelling" that is the Zen mind, a mind that is free and at ease.

Creating the will without dwelling means both entering and leaving so that the river of trouble may be crossed and the far bank of ease of mind reached.

* * *

Creating the will without dwelling is the essence of the *Diamond Sutra* and of Zen.

"Not dwelling" is to behave in society so as to transcend the external material world, not to be confused by things and to reach beyond it;

"Creating the will" is to behave in society so as to understand the external material world, to respond to it naturally and to reach beyond it.

Creating the will without dwelling brings vitality to life; not dwelling and creating the will brings tranquillity.

Creating the will without dwelling is like a sword so sharp that it will split a hair floating on the breath. Used skilfully it will bring victory on all sides.

Chapter VIII
Living in the Moment

There was once a man who was being chased through the wild by a tiger. Desperately trying to escape he fell over a cliff. He managed to scramble and grasp hold of a rattan creeper and found himself hanging in mid-air. He looked up and saw the tiger staring at him from above. He looked down and saw the abyss that awaited him below. He looked around and saw, just above the creeper, some ripe strawberries.

He stretched out a hand, picked the strawberries, and put them in his mouth, saying all the while: "Really sweet!" (*Parable Sutra*)

This is the mind-set of living in the moment.

"In the moment" is a complete experience of all moments, including the circumstances of the moment, the moment in time, and the moment in conduct and in feeling.

Keep a Grip of the Immediate

We live in a life of delusions. The well known story of the milkmaid is an example. She walked from field to market with a pail of milk on her head. As she walked she thought of how she could sell the milk and buy eggs, the eggs would hatch chicks that would grow and could be sold at a good price so that she could buy fine clothes. Dressed in fine clothes she could meet Prince Charming after Prince Charming. As she walked and thought, the bucket fell from her head and the milk was spilled, the chickens flew away, the eggs were broken and her dreams were destroyed.

Some people live in the past and some in the future. Both completely ignore the present.

The Zen approach is to live in the moment, neither absorbed by the delusions of the past or of the future, and taking each step in life firmly and with care.

Watch Your Step

Zen master Fa Yan, after chatting with three disciples in a pavilion, returned to his room to rest and found that the lamp was already out.

Fa Yan asked his disciples: "How do you feel at the moment?"

Two of the disciples replied that it was like being in a fog and being unable to find anything. The third, Yuanwu Keqin said: "Watch your step!"

Fa Yan was full of praise for this answer.

When the lamp is out it is as black as lacquer. The way forward and the way back are both unclear. What should we do?

Obviously: "Watch your step, look to the present!"

Many people are superstitiously caught up with the life to come and with previous lives. We blame misfortune in our present life upon the debts of a previous existence; we turn our dissatisfaction with our current life to a hope in the next life, saying that we can wait until the next life for our aspirations to be realised.

The problem is that while we are dreaming about the previous and the next lives we miss the scenery of the moment. We must remember that Zen essential: Watch your step!

Watch your step means that when we eat we should eat properly, when we sleep we should sleep properly, when we work we should work properly and that when we enjoy ourselves we should do so properly.

Do Not Miss the Opportunity of the Moment

Because the past has gone, time does not flow backwards. The future has yet to come and time cannot be bought in advance. Therefore we can only grasp the present. Living in the moment we must treasure today.

Because we can only grasp life today—not yesterday, not tomorrow—it follows that for us, today is the most important day.

Today Is the Most Important Day

A young man sought out a sage deep in the mountains and asked his advice.

"Master, which day of your life is the most important? Is it the day of your birth, or is it the day of your death? Is it the day that you began to study or the day of your enlightenment?"

The sage immediately responded: "None of them, the most important day of life is today."

The young man asked curiously: "Why is that? Do you mean to say something earth-shattering has happened today?"

"Nothing has happened today."

"Then why do you say that it is important?"

The sage said: "Because today is the only day that we have. Yesterday, however worthy of recall, is like a boat that has sunk to the bottom of the ocean: tomorrow, however glorious, has not yet arrived. Today, however ordinary, is within our grasp and in our control."

The young man wished to continue asking questions but the sage stopped him, saying: "In discussing its importance we have already wasted our today!"

The young man, as if something had suddenly occurred to him, flew down the mountain as fast as his feet could carry him.

Zen tells us: if someone thinks constantly about yesterday or is always worried and anxious about tomorrow, they will be as dried out as straw.

There are people who constantly regret the passing of the years, there are those who spend their days in vain hopes for the future. They all overlook the significance of today.

Life is temporary, its affairs are impermanent and nobody knows what may occur tomorrow. We can only live in today and must spend it conscientiously, treasuring every moment.

Cherish the Process

Life is a process and not merely a result. If we care too much about the result we are in danger of overlooking the joy of the process.

Life is so busy and exhausting that however beautiful the passing scenery we cannot spare it a glance, so that the days drag by.

This kind of life is like a hurried journey in which each stop passes rapidly:

When young we break our necks thinking about getting into a better school;

Then we long to graduate and obtain a good job;

Then we rush to marry and raise a family;

Then we long for our children to grow up quickly and relieve us of a mental burden;

Then when they are grown up we can't wait to retire.

So it goes on and on, and when we do really retire we suddenly discover that we are old, and that when we want to rest and take a breath and enjoy life, we are already at death's door!

In truth, many of life's joys are to be found in the actual process of life. Viewed through the eyes of Zen, each stage of the journey is in itself an objective. This is known as "Not leaving home while on a journey." (*Record of the Sayings of Renowned Monks*)

The "journey" is work undertaken for the realisation of a certain objective; "home" is our destination. If we regard "journey" as "home" we can eliminate the element of external objective and experience the pleasure of the work itself.

The wise are skilled at discovering the joy within the process of life, and becoming artists in living.

On the River in the Snow, The Stringless *Qin*[1]

The fifth century collection of sayings, *A New Miscellany*, records the tale of the East Jin literary figure Wang Huizhi of Shanyin, son of the great calligrapher Wang Xizhi. One night, when snow was falling and nothing could be seen but an expanse of white, Wang Huizhi suddenly thought of his good friend Dai Kui and in high spirits ordered a boat and set off to visit him. The marvel of this tale is that it turns the process itself into the result. It was in the process of visiting a friend on a night of falling snow that Wang Huizhi discovered real joy.

Wang Huizhi lived at Shanyin, near Shaoxing

---

[1]Chinese stringed musical instrument from around 2500 BC.

in present day Zhejiang province. Dai Kui lived at Shanxi in Sheng county, also in present day Zhejiang. These two places are 200 *li* distant from each other by river. Moreover the journey was against the current and to cover the distance in a night required the assistance of a strong north-west wind.

We can imagine how high Wang Huizhi's spirits must have been to brave the snow, ice and the wind.

What was even more astonishing was the fact that on the morning of the second day, having, with some difficulty, reached the entrance to his friend's house, Wang Huizhi made the surprising decision not to land and visit his old friend, but told his attendants to order the boatman to take the boat back.

Everybody was curious and asked him why he had done this. Wang Huizhi said: "I came on an impulse and am returning on an impulse. What need to see Dai?"

This is the simple beauty of the intoxicating so-called Wei-Jin lifestyle.

The value of the beauty lies in the process itself and

not in any external objective or aim.

Another well known figure of the Jin dynasty was the poet Tao Yuanming who possessed a similar style. He had a *qin* which had not been strung, nor could he play the *qin* himself. When tipsy he liked to strum the instrument and was completely intoxicated by the beauty of the imaginary sounds that he heard.

Happy in the Moment

There is a Zen saying: "Strive to view the moon in heaven and lose the pearl in your hand." (*Compendium of Five Lamps*) "The moment" is the pearl and the distant objective the moon in the sky.

To live happily in the moment one should joyfully concentrate one's interests in the moment and experience them wholeheartedly.

We live in a hurry and no matter what it is—eating, walking, sleeping—we never have any patience. We are always rushing urgently towards the next objective, never able to turn our attention towards the moment, always thinking of tomorrow, or next year or the rest of our life.

People say: "Next year, I'm going to earn more." Others say: "I'm going to get a larger house" and yet others: "I'm going to get a higher position."

Later, they earn more, have larger houses and gain rapid promotion but they are still unhappy and dissatisfied, thinking: "I should earn a little more, my house should be a bit bigger and my position a little higher!"

This is to have lost the immediate and not to live in the moment. With this kind of mindset there can be no happiness since we are never satisfied and life becomes one headlong rush, heedless of anything except the way forward.

In fact, there is no need to earn so much more before taking a rest. If our thoughts are always directed towards the future and we have scant regard for the present we shall never be happy. We can only truly possess the moment. The future is out of our hands.

What is happiness in life? It is the sunshine of the moment.

The bright, warm sunshine is there every day. You may enjoy it as much as you like as long as you avoid distraction and concentrate on the moment. Then, your face will be warmed by it.

Once this mystery is fathomed, even an ordinary person may understand how to live better than a philosopher.

The Happy Fisherman

A philosopher saw a fisherman taking the sun on a beach and asked: "Why aren't you fishing?"

The fisherman said: "I've already brought back a catch."

The philosopher said: "Why don't you catch another boatload?"

The fisherman said: "I have enough to eat and enough for my needs already."

The philosopher said: "If you caught more you would earn more from selling them."

The fisherman shook his head: "What would I want all that money for?"

The philosopher reckoned on his fingers: "If you caught an extra boatload a day, in fifteen years you could buy a lot of boats."

The fisherman said lazily: "What's the use of that?"

The philosopher said seriously: "By then, you could take your ease and lie sunbathing on the beach."

The fisherman said: "But aren't I already lying at ease on the beach sunbathing? And now, revered philosopher, sir, be so good as to move aside and stop blocking my sun."

It can be seen from this that sunlight exists in any place and at any time. The key is whether or not you are in the frame of mind to enjoy it. Happiness too is there and readily available.

* * *

Zen says: "Life is lived in the breath of the moment." Living in the moment we have control of life.

Yesterday's day cannot linger and how many tomorrows will there be? To grasp today is to grasp life.

The most precious things in life are not unattainable or already lost but are present and to be grasped in the moment. With a grip of each minute and each second of the moment, every day can be one of joy and fulfilment.

Grasp the circumstances of the present and treasure the joy of today. Enjoy the process of life and be happy in the moment.

Chapter IX
Who Holds You in Bondage?

At his moment of enlightenment Sakyamuni said: "All sentient beings possess the wisdom and virtuous aspects of the Buddha but because of delusions and attachments cannot manifest them." (*Sayings of Dahui*)

Since delusions and attachments have over-shadowed the original mind and true nature, they must be jettisoned so that one's original sense of enlightenment may re-emerge. As seen by Zen, they are not external but come from the heart. We are like silkworms endlessly spinning out threads of affliction and desire into a thick cocoon, an attachment that rigidly encases us.

Delusions and attachments tie us and that is loss.

Jettisoning delusions and attachments and gaining independence is escape.

The *Platform Sutra* says: "Comprehend and all sentient beings become Buddha. Fail to comprehend and Buddha then becomes as all."

The states of enlightenment and bewilderment are the products of our own mind.

Binding and Release Derive from the Same Mind

The *Surangama Sutra* says:

In bondage and release there is no second one.

Bondage and release are the products of the same mind.

The *Vimalakirti Sutra* says:

If there is bondage then there is release, if, at root, there is no bondage from whom should one seek release?

If bondage exists, then its opposite, escape must also exist. If we know that bondage derives from our inner mind, then there is immediate release and there is no need to seek release elsewhere.

We are bound and released by ourselves, not by others.

What Goes Round and Round?

There was a graduate who went to visit a Zen master at a temple. On his way, he saw an ox tied to a tree by its nose. The ox wanted to graze but was unable to do so because it was tethered with a rope and so circled endlessly round and round the tree. The graduate thought that when he reached the temple he would test the Zen master by asking him whether he could guess what he had seen on the way.

The graduate reached the temple and exchanged greetings, drank tea and chatted with the Zen master. When the two men were relaxed the graduate suddenly asked: "Master, what goes round and round? What goes round in circles?"

The graduate carefully watched the master's reaction as he asked the question, thinking that the master was bound to invoke some magical power to see what he had met on the way. Who would have thought that the very moment that the question left his mouth, the master replied without even thinking:

"It was only because the rope didn't break!"

The graduate was astonished and turned pale, asking: "How did you know that's what I saw and it was because the rope didn't break?"

The master burst into laughter and told him: "What you asked was a physical question. My reply was metaphysical, at a level of truth and of wisdom.

"Just think, why is it that people spend their whole lives going round in circles? It is because they are tied by the nose with a rope that tethers their spirit. Because they do not escape its bonds, they go round in circles."

The graduate listened and prostrated himself in admiration, praising the master's outstanding wisdom.

Are we tethered to things in our lives?

We are slaves to wealth and like making money, so we are tethered to money.

We are slaves to property and like houses, so we are tethered to houses.

We are slaves to lust, and indulge in lechery, so it is lechery that tethers us.

Buddha says that there are 84,000 afflictions. These afflictions are like so many ropes tethering us. Trussed up by ourselves, when are we going to be able to stop going round in circles?

If we wish for a life that is happy and at ease we have to escape this invisible rope.

It's All in the Mind

The *Awakening of Faith*, one of the classic Zen texts says: "All phenomena are born of the mind and extinguished by the mind."

We can only become aware of the existence of things through the mind. So, if there is light in our mind we will see light. If we have demons in our mind, then we will see demons.

Master Wonhyo of Silla

In the period of the late Three Kingdoms in Korea, the great Zen Master Wonhyo (617 – 686) appeared. Out of admiration of the great Chinese Buddhist monk and translator Xuanzang, he decided to accompany his friend, Zen master Uisang, to study Buddhism in China.

Wonhyo and Uisang travelled a long road and, because they were in a hurry, missed a village and were forced to spend a night in a dark wood. It was summer, the dry food they had eaten had made them thirsty and there was not a drop of water in their waterskins.

Wonhyo recalled that they had just passed a bamboo grove from the side of which there had been a watery reflection and the sound of frogs. He guessed that there must be water in the vicinity and set off to find it. It was dark and he couldn't see. He followed the sound of the frogs and, as expected, found a pond. His hand inadvertently knocked against a gourd. He used the gourd to scoop up water and drank his fill thinking the water cool and sweet.

Wishing to share the benefit with his friend, he filled the waterskin and took it back for Uisang.

Uisang drank his fill at one go and said appreciatively: "Who would have thought that in such an out of the way place the water would be so good!"

The next morning they decided to visit the pool to wash and refill their waterskins before taking to the road. When they reached the pool they suddenly saw that there was a skeleton lying in the water and that the gourd was its skull.

The two vomited on the spot at the very sight of it. In that moment, Wonhyo recalled the phrase from the *Awakening of Faith*:

> All phenomena are born of the mind
> and extinguished by the mind.

He had read this text before but without any deep understanding of it. This time, however, Wonhyo had a profound grasp of it.

The water in the pond was still the original water and had not altered. It was his own mind that had altered. Self had believed that the water was clean, sweet and drinkable and self had believed that it was filthy and had immediately vomited it up.

After being sick the two of them continued on their journey. A little later they ran into a rainstorm and splashed their way to shelter. They discovered a large earthen structure by the road, rather like the kilns used by the hill people, and rushed inside. Though the cave, with spiders' webs at its entrance, was rather dilapidated, they felt that finding shelter from the rain was a blessing in the midst of misfortune.

They slept soundly through the night.

At dawn next morning they were shocked to

find that the shelter was not a cave but a huge tomb filled with white bones. They were at once filled with fear and foreboding and wanted to leave.

The wind and rain continued, there was no way that they could leave and they had to spend another night in the tomb.

This time, they did not sleep as well as they had done the previous night. They seemed to hear the shrieking of ghosts and saw countless apparitions. Demons howled everywhere. They spent an uncomfortable night tossing and turning.

On the third morning as the warm sunshine flooded into the cave, Wonhyo attained a complete realization of the principle that lay behind "All phenomena are born of the mind and extinguished by the mind."

It was the mind that had changed, not the external world. When the mind was calm, sleep was sound; when it was agitated, sleep was disturbed.

After these two events, Wonhyo achieved a sudden flash of enlightenment. He had come to an understanding of the basic spirit of Zen and had realized the secrets of life. There was no longer any need to visit the venerable monks of China and he returned to Silla and became one of the founders of Buddhism in Korea.

One Mind Opens Two Doors

The *Awakening of Faith* contains an important concept, that of "one mind opens two doors."

"One mind" refers to our own mind. The "two doors" refers to the "door of things as they are," the mind of sentient beings or suchness, and to the "door of birth and death." The door of things as they are, *zhenru men*, is enlightenment, the pure tranquillity of the mind. The door of birth and death is fantasy, where thoughts are in constant circulation and trammelled by desire.

The significance of one mind two doors is that it brings us to recognise the following principle:

In a state of enlightenment we possess a pure mind, the mind of the door of things as they are; in a state of bewilderment our mind is impure and is the mind of the door of birth and death.

Throughout life, even during the course of a single day, we go in and out of these two doors, one moment enlightened and the next unable to withstand temptation.

It can be seen from this that the origins of joy and suffering and the causes of uprightness and depravity lie only in our own minds.

The nurture of this mind leads to instant enlightenment.

It is the mind that determines whether you go to heaven or hell.

Heaven and Hell

A samurai once asked the 18th century Japanese Zen master Hakuin: "I've read many scriptures which all say that there is a heaven and a hell. May I ask you whether there really is a heaven and hell?"

Hakuin immediately knew where the nub of the problem lay and deciding to use a Zen technique to enlighten him asked: "What are you?"

"I'm a samurai."

"You're a samurai?" Hakuin bellowed, "What stupid master could ask you to be his bodyguard? Look at you, you sloppy, rat-faced thief. You look like nothing so much as a beggar!"

"What are you saying?" The samurai, his blood up, leaped to his feet, his hand on the sword at his waist. A samurai may be prepared to lose his life but he will always protect his reputation.

Hakuin continued scornfully: "What are you going to draw your sword for? This old monk's body of mine is as hard as a diamond. That useless piece of iron of yours won't split my skull!"

Unable to bear it anymore, the samurai drew his sword and with hatred in his eyes was on the point of striking at Hakuin.

Hakuin looked calmly at the samurai and quietly said: "The gates of hell are open now!"

The samurai heard and broke into a cold sweat of terror. He knew that the Zen master was a man of compassion who had roused his own ignorant anger as a means of enlightenment. He sensed the risk that he had taken and realised the strength of the Zen master's practice of Zen. Throwing down his sword he knelt before the monk in apology.

Hakuin smiled and warmly told the samurai: "Now, the gate to heaven is open!"

An evil angry thought leads to hell; a thought corrected by remorse leads to heaven.

Heaven and hell are not places that you go to when you die, they exist in our every thought in every moment.

Whether we go to heaven or hell, towards light or dark, into bewilderment or liberation is completely determined by our own mind. To realize the wisdom of Zen we must look after our own mind and prevent it from entering the wrong door.

Being Mortal or Immortal

It is difficult to become a Buddha but becoming a devil is the matter of a moment because we are always at a crossroads, always faced with, and in the midst of, decisions.

The devilish side of human nature tempts us all the time: when we know it's wrong we do it anyhow; when we know it's right we are unwilling to persevere. Many decisions are the false step of a moment. These are known as "Between Buddha and demon the idea of an instant." For example, because of a false step in a quarrel someone may, through a sudden surge of evil, knife somebody; somebody else may lose self-control in the face of wealth and corruptly misappropriate public funds.

It is precisely because of this hair's breadth instant of thought between Buddha and demon that the Zen classic the *Diamond Sutra* strongly emphasises the need to "guard every thought with virtue" and to take care of every idea.

If we let go of our mind, it will degenerate; but if we care for it, it can transcend the mortal, become immortal (become an Arhat) and achieve a higher stage of life.

Zen says that "the demon mind is devilish and the Buddha mind Buddha-like." Becoming a Buddha or a demon is the matter of a moment.

Buddha or Demon Are Creations of Self

There was an artist who wanted to depict Buddha and demons. In order to make his picture more lifelike he wanted to find a model in reality but never found one and finally gave up.

By chance, when he was making an offering of incense in a temple, he noticed a monk of a serene and dignified demeanour that attracted him and whom he sought out and asked to be a model. Hearing that the artist wanted him as a model so as to help him depict a Buddha the monk happily agreed.

When the work was completed it had a sensational effect. The artist said with conceit: "This is the most satisfactory picture that I have ever done because when people looked at the model, they believed him to be a Buddha. His demeanor moved everybody!"

This picture brought great success to the artist and in order to express his thanks, he made a gift of a large sum of money to the monk.

A year later the artist was preparing to do a picture of a demon. A similar problem arose however. Where could he find a model for a demon?

He travelled everywhere and sought out evil looking people but none of them satisfied him. Eventually he found someone in prison who was the spitting image of the demon of his imagination.

The artist was delighted and thought that he could achieve another masterpiece with this model.

However, when the criminal saw him he wept and said: "Why is it that the last time when you painted a Buddha it was me that you chose and this time when you are painting a demon it's me again! You've turned me from a Buddha to a demon!"

The artist said in surprise: "How is this possible? The man I portrayed was of no ordinary demeanor and you seem to be an out-and-out devil. How can you be the same person?"

The man replied dejectedly: "Ever after I

had that money from you, all I thought of was pleasure and enjoyment. I spent extravagantly on the vices of wine, women and gambling. There was nothing that I didn't indulge in. Finally I became a drug addict. Eventually I ran out of money but my craving was uncontrollable. I went and stole some money but killed somebody during the robbery. I would do anything for money. In the beginning I still had a sense of shame but later on I was completely insensitive and became what I am now!"

The artist heard this with deep regret. To his utter surprise the two completely opposite schemes of creating a Buddha and a demon had come together in the same body!

Although the major cause of the transformation lay in the man's own inability to curb his greed, the artist felt that he bore an inescapable responsibility. He threw his brushes away and never painted again.

* * *

Bewilderment and enlightenment are determined by our own minds.

We both bind ourselves and liberate ourselves.

If there is sunlight in our hearts we can see light in the depths of darkness; if our mind is in shadow we will see ghosts in daylight.

Virtue of mind and thought leads to heaven. Wickedness of thought and mind is the road to hell.

It is our mind that determines whether we become mortal or immortal, a Buddha or a demon.

Most of all, as we live in this world, it is critical that we look after our own mind.

Chapter X
Take Good Care of Your Mind

We live in a world of rapid change where, for many, the pressures of life cause physical and mental exhaustion and where "depression" has become a contemporary catchword. For the contemporary person, the universal mood is one of anxiety, boredom, despair and loneliness that breeds mental illness, and an increasing incidence of suicide.

Despair has forced many to waste precious lives on a journey of no return. In this situation, what can the wisdom of Zen do to help?

Where mind and circumstance are concerned, the distinction between the wise and the ignorant is:

> In the state of delusion circumstance controls mind, in enlightenment mind controls circumstance. (*Zongjinglu*)

The inner minds of the ignorant are controlled by the

external. This is "circumstance controls mind." The wise use the mind to control and alter external circumstances. This is "mind controls circumstance."

"Circumstance controls mind" represents the state of delusion.

"Mind controls circumstance" represents the state of enlightenment .

Using the mind to change circumstances alters our perception of the external world by changing our state of mind. This is the essence of Zen.

Fatality by Shadow

Plato said that the greatest mistake of doctors was that they only healed the body and not the mind. Whereas, in fact, mind and body are a whole and should not be dealt with separately. It has taken 2,300 years for the medical profession to realise this truth. It was only in the last century that the new study of psychophysiology was developed to treat both body and mind.

In medical practice the phenomenon of "suicide by thought" (*yinian zisha*) is attracting more and more attention.

The Death of the Little White Mouse

An American journal has published an account of a psychological experiment involving the study of the behavior of a white mouse in water under dangerous conditions.

The swimming ability of mice is highly developed. When the mouse was placed in a pool of water it did not immediately start to swim but went round and round emitting squeaks. It was fixing its position. The whiskers of mice are directional indicators and the mouse's squeaks were reflected by the edge of the pool back to the whiskers, thus allowing the mouse to judge the direction and distance of its target. The mouse circled several times emitting squeaks, chose a direction and started swimming vigorously. Within moments it had reached the bank. This test was repeated a number of times with the same result.

Subsequently, the mouse's whiskers were clipped and it was placed in the center of the pool again. It swam in circles squeaking as before but lacking whiskers was unable to fix its position. It continued squeaking and circling in agitation until it sank and drowned.

What was it that led to the mouse's death? It was because the mouse, deprived of its whiskers was unable to fix its position, so that in its mind it was surrounded by a vast sheet of water with no way of escape. In this situation it ceased all effort. It could also be said that the mouse was dead before it drowned.

The psychologist concluded that on the premise that there is absolutely no hope, all animals will take their own lives. This is known as "suicide by thought."

An incorrect perception of the external world can easily lead to negative thoughts. These thoughts can make a white mouse take its own life.

In real life, therefore, when reverses and desperation cause fear and despair, we must escape despair by adjusting our state of mind and positively transforming it to a state of active optimism .

Transforming the External Environment by Mind

The *Vimalakirti Sutra* says:

If the mind is pure, the land is pure also.

So-called "cultivation" is the revision of one's own behavior that is determined by our mind. Therefore "cultivation" actually means the cultivation of the mind. If the mind is clean then the environment in which we live will be clean too and a place of joy. In our eyes everyone will be decent, everywhere will be fine and everything all right.

There is a Chinese saying "the sick clam produces a pearl" which illustrates this problem.

When sand gets into a clam, the clam feels intensely uncomfortable but has no way of getting rid of the sand. It now faces two choices: one is to live in discomfort; the other is to seek a means of transforming the grain of sand so that both can live in peaceful co-existence.

The clam adopts the second course and uses part of its nutrition to envelop the grain of sand after which it considers it part of its own body and no longer an outsider. The more the grain of sand consumes the clam's nutrition the more the clam considers it part of itself and the more it lives harmoniously with it.

In this way, the clam, from its initial feeling of extreme discomfort changes to a state of living in harmony with the grain of sand and eventually turns it into a pearl.

The clam is an invertebrate without a brain and very low on the ladder of evolution. Nevertheless, it knows how to cope with an environment that it cannot change and is able to transform an unpleasant alien presence into a part of itself that it can accommodate and with which it can co-exist.

Mankind "the king of all things" is, in this respect, no better than the clam and should be ashamed of its title.

Let us now look at how the Zen wisdom of using the mind to transform the (external) world can be used in practice.

The Woman Who Willed
Her Own Abandonment

There was a woman, so beautiful that the birds tumbled from the heavens and the moon was put to shame, who loved her husband dearly. Unfortunately, she was dogged by that cruel fate which often attaches to beautiful and talented women. No matter how tender and how kind she had been she was abandoned by her heartless husband.

Weeping tears of misery she went to a Zen master and said: "Master, I am suffering greatly, I have suffered so much with this misfortune that I can take no more. How can I live this life?"

The Zen master remained silent, and the woman wept even more bitterly, on and on without end.

In order to try and induce her to see things in a different light, the Zen master slapped the table and shouted assertively: "As far as I can see, it was not your husband who abandoned you but you who willingly abandoned him!"

As if she had had a bucket of cold water thrown over her, the woman rushed to reply: "Master, I am to be pitied, how can you say that I willingly abandoned him when I have suffered such misfortune, how can it be possible!"

The master said: "Just think a moment, I very much sympathise with you in what has happened. But this misfortune is in the past and should be let pass, you mustn't spend every day mulling over it from morn till night. Before you were married did not the sun shine brightly on your life? Your husband was heartless and that such a man has left you shows that your affinity had run its course and is a matter for congratulation. Zen says that having been struck by the arrow of another you should not then loose another arrow at yourself.

When you have been harmed by somebody else on no account must you esteem yourself any the less! At the moment somebody else has fired an arrow at you but you persist in poking at the wound with a knife, aren't you being unfair on yourself?

"If you go on about this all day and every day it will become more and more serious and like a mountain it will overwhelm you. Let me calculate for you: there are 365 days in a year, if you go on about it once a day that means that you will have been abandoned 365 times in a year; if you do it ten times in a day, that means that he will have abandoned you 3,650 times. Is this what you really want?"

The woman immediately came to a great understanding.

What had she realised?

You cannot change your environment but you can change yourself;

You cannot change events but you can change your attitude to them;

You cannot change the past but you can change the present!

Faced with a similar situation employing the Zen

wisdom of "using mind to transform the external world" the event could be transcended and faced calmly. Faced with an every day pattern of thought however it becomes a matter of great suffering.

In truth, this is the way life is, when we approach things with a different mental attitude, the landscape and the realm change.

Move Forward Optimistically

An important Zen truth is that only by improving ourselves and our attitudes can we make any headway. If we adopt an optimistic attitude we can move forward in confidence and give full play to our potential in all the exams that life sets us and obtain the best results.

The Provincial Graduate's Three Dreams
A provincial graduate who wished to attend the imperial examinations in the capital had three dreams. The first was that he was planting cabbage on the top of a wall. The second, that in the rain he was wearing both a bamboo raincoat and carrying an umbrella. The third was that he was sleeping in the bridal chamber with the girl that he yearned

after, but back-to-back.

He asked a Daoist priest to interpret the dreams for him. The Daoist said: "Wretched graduate that you are, these three dreams of yours are really bad luck. The cabbages on the wall are a waste of time; the umbrella and the raincoat in the rain are superfluous; and as to sleeping back-to-back in the bridal chamber with the girl you love, it's useless to think of that as a sign of a successful conclusion. You'd best not take the imperial exams but pack your bags and go home!"

The graduate was downcast and prepared to leave. On the way he met a Zen master and described to him what had happened.

The Zen master clapped his hands and laughed: "Congratulations, you will be top of the list!"

The graduate said: "You really are a joker. I'm miserable, yet you make a joke of me."

The Zen master replied: "As I see it, it's completely the other way round. If you think about it, planting cabbages on the top of the wall means that you are planting higher than others and will get a higher result! Both umbrella and raincoat mean that your preparations have been adequate, a double insurance. As for sleeping in the bridal chamber with the girl you love, although back-to-back, you just have to turn round for a successful conclusion. This demonstrates that your success will be doubled, your dreams will come true and that the time to turn round is about to arrive!"

The graduate was delighted, cast off his mental burden and as the Zen master said he would, at one stroke achieved the highest place in the exams.

The cause of the way in which the graduate completely turned his life around was an attitude of Zen joy formed by a strong internal stimulus. Had he been influenced by the first interpretation, his attitude would have been one of "I'll never pass, I'm bound to fail." He would have been unable to answer the simplest question because he had already caused himself to fail before he entered the examination hall. Conversely, encouraged by the second interpretation and taking the exam in a spirit of "I'm going to succeed and come top" he was able to realise his maximum potential and achieve a result beyond the normal standard. He had already psychologically come top before the exam.

The influence of mental attitude upon the external

world is so great that it can not only bring success to our ordinary lives but it can also be our spiritual mainstay in living through and beyond despair.

Zen tells us:

> The world is changed by the mind, the world never departs the mind. (*Zongjinglu*)

We must utilise this wisdom to transform the world in a mood of positive optimism. If the landscape that faces us is dull then our mind can change it to one of beauty. If our life is one of regret our mind can transform it into one of bliss.

* * *

The mindset of the ignorant follows the external world and is influenced by it. Dominated by the external world it leads to fear, dejection and pessimism. These actively negative attitudes can cause a person to collapse into utter despair and even catastrophe.

The wise must throw off the bonds of the external world and transform their view of it through a change in attitude.

Viewed with an attitude of Zen joy the world is bright

with hope.

By cultivating an attitude of Zen joy we can transcend suffering and regret, thereby bringing happiness and confidence to our lives.

Chapter XI
Seeing the World with Eyes of Zen Joy

Three bricklayers were building a wall. A philosopher asked: "What are you doing?"

The first replied: "Building a wall."

The second replied: "Putting up a building."

The third replied: "We are building our home."

The philosopher clapped the third man on the shoulder and said: "You will be fortunate in the future."

Many years later the first bricklayer was still a bricklayer. The second had become an engineer and the third was the boss of the other two.

All three possessed the attitude of Zen joy. This attitude means employing the wisdom of Zen to use the mind to change the environment and transform affliction, transcend difficulty and achieve a mental state of calm happiness.

Seen with an attitude of Zen joy the world is bright.

Attitude Is the Root

The attitude of Zen joy can reduce stress, build self-confidence, fulfil potential and embrace the world.

It is not that the world is without oases but that we see desert. If there is bright sunshine in our mind there can be no darkness in the world.

With an attitude of Zen joy life will be bathed in sunshine.

The Millennium Competition

At the beginning of the century, a magazine launched a competition under the title "What I want most from the 21st century," with a prize of 10,000 dollars.

Nearly 20,000 entries from all over the world flooded in.

The magazine analyzed the entries according to title. Statistics showed that 57% wanted money, 21% wanted a happy family, 8% wanted power and position and 5% wanted a good looking and virtuous wife.

A panel of experts judged the entries with an unexpected result. The winner of the competition was a 300-word article under the title "What

I want most is a positively happy and sunny disposition."

The panel's judgement ran: No matter whether you want money or power, a happy family or a good car and a better house, the possession of a positive, sunny attitude will get you anything. In the world to come attitude will be the basic competitive strength.

Attitude Is Gold

A good attitude leads to success and a bad one to destruction. Consequently, success and happiness require not only an attitude of Zen joy but its cultivation as well.

Our life is made up of countless ordinary matters. With the philosopher's stone of Zen joy, we can turn iron to gold and fill a life built from the ordinary with happiness.

Cow Dung and a Statue of Buddha

The *Vimalakirti Sutra* says:

If the mind is pure, the land is pure also.

If your mind is pure then the world in which you live will be both good and harmonious; if you look upon others as demons then you will live in hell; if you regard them as angels you will dwell in heaven.

One day Su Dongpo visited his friend, the Zen master Fo Yin, to take tea. They sat cross-legged tasting the tea and talking.

"What do you think I look like?" Su Dongpo asked.

Fo Yin replied: "I think you look like a Buddha."

Su Dongpo smiled and said: "Well, I think you look like a pile of cow dung!"

Fo Yin smiled and said nothing.

Su Dongpo thought that on this occasion he had won and scored a point at little cost. He went home and with immense self-satisfaction regaled his sister with the story.

His sister said: "Brother, you've lost! It's your attitude that determines what you see. The fact that Master Fo Yin said that you looked like a Buddha demonstrates that he has a Buddha-like mind. The fact that you said he looked like a pile of cow dung demonstrates that your mind contains a dung heap!"

Su Dongpo blushed and realised that in this verbal contest with Zen master Fo Yin he had come off worst.

We can see from this exchange that attitude determines how you behave. If your mind is full of dung then you will look on others as dung. If Buddha is in your mind then you will regard everybody as a Buddha.

It is our mind that determines the world we see: if we look at the world sorrowfully we see gloom and despondency; if our disposition is sunny then we see a world of bright sunlight.

Before his enlightenment Zen master Baoji of Panshan passed by a market. A customer was buying pork and said to the butcher: "Cut me a catty of your prime meat!" The butcher thereupon cut him a catty of prime meat. However the customer was fussy and kept complaining of the fat and picking out the lean, all the time demanding prime cuts. Eventually, the butcher could put up with it no longer, thrust his knife into the chopping block, put his hands on his hips and yelled: "What are you being so fussy about, which

of these pieces is not prime?" Speak carefully lest
offence be taken. Baoji heard and was suddenly
enlightened. (*Compendium of Five Lamps*)

We are fussy in life, but once we rid ourselves of
a sense of difference—"which of these pieces is not
prime?"—there will be sunlight everywhere.

Optimism Increases Self-Confidence

The French author Victor Hugo once said: "Ideas may
turn heaven to hell and hell to heaven." The function of
the attitude of Zen joy is to transform hell into heaven.

The Professor's Experiment

During the 1960s a professor conducted a famous
experiment in a high school. The new school
year had just started and the professor asked the
school principal to invite two of the teachers into
the office, where he told them: "On the basis of
your teaching record you are the best teachers in
the school. Consequently, we are selecting 100 of
the brightest pupils and forming them into two
classes that you will then teach. The I.Q.s of these

students are higher than those of other children and we hope that you will be able to achieve even better grades."

The two teachers were pleased to hear this and indicated that they would do all they could to enable these children to make even better progress.

A year later, the results of these two classes were way ahead of the rest of the school. At this point the professor told the teachers the truth: their students were not specially chosen children of high intelligence but merely ordinary students randomly selected.

The two teachers, speechless, looked at each other in utter surprise. They had no idea that this was the situation and concluded that their standard of teaching was actually quite high. The professor then told them a further truth: they had not been specially selected teachers of superior ability either, but ordinary teachers randomly chosen.

In this experiment both teachers believing that they were outstanding and that the students all had a high I.Q. boosted their self-confidence through auto-suggestion thereby nurturing a state of Zen joy. This led to more energetic and confident teaching of their students and a bumper harvest of results.

Shed Light Everywhere

Seen through the state of Zen joy the world is bright since those who possess the quality of Zen joy are able to see light and ignore darkness.

Everywhere Is Good

In a state of Zen joy you will discover that every place is a good place. Plato said: "A man's mood is determined not by his circumstances but by his state of mind." If we are in a good mood, joy is to be found wherever we are.

There was a philosopher who lived with several friends in a room only a few feet square. He was always happy and someone asked him: "With so many people squeezed together, what have you to be happy about?" He replied: "Living with friends I can exchange ideas and enjoy a good relationship with them, of course I'm happy."

In the course of time, all his friends got married and moved out leaving him living by himself, but he was as happy as ever. Again, someone asked him: "Living by yourself, what's there to be happy about?" The philosopher replied: "I have a lot of books, each one is a friend and teacher, how can I not be happy in their company?"

Several years later the philosopher married and had a family and was given the ground floor in which to live. He was still as cheerful as ever. He was asked: "The ground floor is so noisy how can you be so happy here?" He replied: "Living on the ground floor is really good! The moment I go in I'm with my family and it's convenient for going in and out and for going for walks. On the ground floor I can grow grass and flowers on any spare ground as well."

No matter where this philosopher lived, in his home the sun shone brightly because his mind was filled with sunlight.

* * *

Of the greatest value in the 21st century is a positive attitude of Zen joy.

Our lives will be determined by our state of mind.

A state of Zen joy can turn iron to gold and bring sunshine to our lives.

Once possessed of a state of Zen joy each place in life is a good place, every event a good one and every person a good person.

In a state of Zen joy we can calmly emerge from darkness, escape from despair and climb out of the dry wells of life.

Chapter XII
Climbing Out of the Well

There was a peasant who had a donkey that stumbled into a dry well. The peasant racked his brains for a means of rescuing it, but without success. Time passed and the donkey was still braying mournfully. The peasant abandoned the idea of rescuing it and listening to the dreadful sounds it was making, decided in desperation to ask his neighbors to help him bury the donkey in the well and put an end to its suffering.

Everybody started to shovel earth into the well and the donkey brayed plaintively as it realised the plight it was in. After a while, however, it calmed down. By the time that everybody thought the donkey was more or less buried, they heard it bray once and saw it climb out of the mouth of the well and disappear like a puff of smoke.

When the earth had started to fall on its back, the donkey had repeatedly shaken it off, trodden it underfoot and clambered on to it until finally it was able to escape.

The wisdom of Zen lies in shaking off the earth of affliction and climbing out of the well.

Achieving Maturity Is Not Comfortable

There were once two blocks of stone, indistinguishable from each other. Later, fate decreed a great change. One block was worshipped and respected and the other ignored and trodden underfoot.

The one that was worshipped was carved into a statue of a Buddha; the one that was trodden on was laid as part of the paving in front of the great hall.

The paving stone bore a grudge against fate for being unfair and said: "We were both more or less the same, why is it that you get worshipped and I get trodden on?" The other stone said: "Do you know the reason that they worship me and tread on you? I suffered the pain of a thousand and more cuts when, slice by slice, I was carved into a statue. You're afraid of the pain of being cut slice by slice, so all you can do is to lie there being trampled on by the multitudes!"

There can be no achievement without the experience of suffering.

Life is like the plum blossom that only emits its fragrance after a hard winter.

Tea and Temperature

A disappointed young man made the long journey to visit the Zen residence of Mountain and Water at Zhongnan Hill to call on the Zen master Ming Xin. He said dejectedly: "Life is not as I had hoped. Everything is at sixes and sevens, full of affliction and suffering and really without meaning. Better to put an end to it all."

The Zen master listened quietly to the young man's sighs of dissatisfaction and instructed an attendant: "Our visitor has come a long way, please bring some warm water."

The attendant soon returned with the warm water. The Zen master put tea leaves into a bowl and added the water. The tightly curled leaves floated gently on the surface of the water, giving no sign of uncurling.

The young man was puzzled and asked: "Master, why are you making tea with warm water?"

The master smiled and said nothing. The young man took a mouthful of tea, shook his head and said: "It doesn't taste like tea at all."

The Zen master said: "But this is good Iron Buddha tea."

The master then instructed the attendant: "Go and get some boiling water."

After a while the young monk came back with a pot of boiling water. The master took another bowl, put in the tea and added the water.

Once the tea leaves were covered with boiling water an intense fragrance drifted up from the bowl.

The master said with a smile: "Our guest knows that this is the same Iron Buddha tea, but why is its flavor so completely different?"

The young man said thoughtfully: "Because of the difference in the temperature of the water used to make the tea."

"Quite right, when tea is made with warm water, the leaves float on the surface so how can they give off their fragrance? When boiling water is used it releases the fragrance.

"It's the same with the places where tea is grown. The same with Wulong tea which is generally grown close to sea level where variations in temperature are not great; Wulong tea grown higher in the hills, experiences greater variations in temperature so that its value is four or five times that of ordinary Wulong tea.

"Why should we ordinary mortals be any different? Without experiencing tempest and storm we are like tea leaves in warm water that cannot release their fragrance and can only float on the surface. Only those who have experienced the storms of life, like tea leaves in boiling water changing as they rise and fall, can finally release that intoxicating flavor."

Life is like a tea leaf that has to be steeped in boiling water before it releases its flavor. The harsh world in which we live may seem a torment. In reality it is an achievement.

Contrariwise, comfortable surroundings can sap the will and cause an unconscious loss of determination that is a waste of life.

Comfort Is Not Maturity

Each one of us likes ease and enjoyment, but there has to be moderation. The *Book of Rites* says: "Joy should not be excessive or desire over-indulged." Mencius said:

Man lives through suffering and dies of ease.

These quotations warn us against indulgence in enjoyment, and in particular against over-indulgence. The Song dynasty Zen master Fa Yan said: "Good fortune is not to be enjoyed to exhaustion." A Chinese folk saying says: "There is no bitterness that may not be tasted but there is fortune that may not be enjoyed."

Many people have become accustomed to a life of prosperity and enjoyment. Viewed scientifically, however, there are many drawbacks to such a life.

Firstly it can lead to nutritional excess and obesity.

An everyday diet of rich food, high in saturated fats and sugars, together with a lack of exercise and a calorific input which exceeds output, leads to nutritional excess. This results in an accumulation of body fat, obesity and a susceptibility to high blood pressure, hardening of the arteries and coronary heart disease.

Secondly it can result in lowered I.Q. and degeneration of the brain.

Evidence shows that a certain tension of the nervous system contributes to physical health by reducing fatigue and strengthening the immune system. Those who lead too easy a life and do not use their brains experience a gradual dulling of the intellect. They appear to lack spirit, are inactive, absent-minded and old before their time.

This kind of over-indulgent life is an overwhelming disaster. The easy life causes frustration and once the experiment is over it leads to lack of effort and the loss of the high standards that might have been attained.

The Frog in Warm Water

There is the widely known story of the boiling frog. The experimenters placed a frog in a vessel containing boiling water. The frog, realising its mortal predicament, saved its life by jumping out.

Half an hour later the frog was placed in a similar vessel filled with cold water and began swimming to and fro.

The experimenters then gradually turned up the heat beneath the water and the frog continued to enjoy the warmth of the slightly warm water. However, by the time it had realised that the water was getting hotter and hotter, that it couldn't stand the temperature and that it needed to jump out to save its life, it was too late.

It may have wanted to jump out but it was

too weak and limp to do so and floated in a daze until it was finally boiled alive.

This experiment sounds inhumane and unethical but it exposes the cruel fact that a life of indulgent ease is exactly the same.

Under pressure we usually fight and often find the unexpected potential to break out. Once we are well known and proud of our success our will becomes paralyzed and amidst a life of extravagance we lose ourselves. What difference is there then between us and the frog that was boiled to death?

Adversity in life is like the frog's boiling water. It may be escaped from in a single bound. The frog's warm water resembles the favorable circumstances of life that are to be feared more than adversity. In favorable circumstances we become paralyzed and drop our guard and by the time we discover the hidden threat the situation is already beyond recall.

Turn Pressure to Motion

When in adversity and under pressure there seems no escape we must turn pressure to movement.

The Antelope and the Jackals

A zoologist who was conducting research into the behavior of antelope herds on both banks of the Orange River in Africa discovered that the reproductive ability of those on the west bank was stronger. At the same time they galloped faster than those on the east bank though their environment and diet were similar.

To confirm his findings he selected ten antelope from each bank and moved them to the opposite bank.

A year later the ten antelopes moved to the east bank had grown to 14 and of the ten moved to the west bank only four remained, the others having been eaten by jackals. The zoologist eventually discovered that the reason for the strength of the herd on the east bank was the presence of a pack of jackals in the vicinity and the weakness of the other herd was caused by the absence of its natural predator.

Animals that lack a natural predator become extinct sooner. Those with a natural predator gradually increase in numbers and strength.

Salvation through Desperation

The American poet James Russell Lowell said: "Mishaps are like knives, that either serve us or cut us, as we grasp them by the blade or by the handle."

In times of difficulty we can cut ourselves if we grasp the blade, but if we grasp the handle it will serve us and we can use it to cut other things.

Galvanising Potential

The majority of great historical figures in China have achieved through trial and tribulation and when in poverty and frustration have, against all odds, produced works that have survived through the ages. The historian Sima Qian (2nd century BC) wrote in his *Reply to Ren An* that a number of major literary or historical works, including the *Book of Changes*, the *Spring and Autumn Annals* and Qu Yuan's poem *Sorrow at Parting* were "the products of righteous anger." He himself said that without having undergone the humiliation of castration he would never have written the *Record of History*, that "ultimate song of the historian."

Escaping from a desperate situation is one of the most effective of Zen training practices. The Korean Zen master whose Chinese name was Hui Qing asked students:

A student of Zen is on a journey when he suddenly finds himself with a deep pit in front of him, a raging forest fire behind him and thorny impenetrable jungle on either side. If he advances he will fall into the pit. If he retreats he will be burned and if he turns to either side he will be impaled on the thorns. How can he avoid catastrophe? (*Compendium of Five Lamps*)

This is designed to make the student see the way back from death in a life-threatening situation where there is no possibility of escape.

Yi Qing, another Zen master adopted a similar method of instruction when he said to his disciples:

Now you're here, move forward and you'll fall into the hands of a demon; move back and you'll be eaten by a hungry ghost; stay still and you'll drown in a pool of stagnant water. How do you get to safety?

This really was a problem from which there was no way out. The disciples thought deeply but failed to grasp the nub of the problem and the Zen hall fell silent. The Zen master laughed and said in enlightenment:

> Three feet of snow cannot crush an inch of spirit! (*Record of Light*)

These two stories explain the same principle. The more dangerous the predicament the more people are able to fulfil their potential and mobilise their powers of comprehension. Three feet of snow cannot crush a pine. There is no road of no return. Whether or not you can escape from desperate straits depends upon how wise you are.

Throughout life everyone needs to face and deal with all kinds of situations. A bright, smooth road through life is, naturally, fine but it may imperceptibly limit the exercise of ability whereas a road that appears hopeless may actually bring out talent.

* * *

Desperation is a psychological dry well, a kind of trial. These wells are impossible to avoid in life. We have to be psychologically prepared before we fall into them. This preparation takes the form of the saying "there is no ease in achievement and no achievement in ease."

No ease in achievement means undergoing the trial of hardships of mind and muscle and the discipline of hard knocks, like the tea leaf that can only emit its fragrance in boiling water.

No achievement in ease, the over-easy life, paralyzes the will like the frog boiled to death. There can be no opportunity to escape if you fall into a well in this state.

We have to realise that many of these so-called desperate situations in life are psychological and that if the psychological issues are resolved we can escape from the well and the situation.

In turning pressure to movement and finding the will to live in a desperate situation we can find salvation through desperation, escape the well, see sunlight again and live a bright, happy life.

Chapter XIII
Seeing Emotion through the Eyes of Zen

Emotions and desire are double-edged swords. Properly managed they can be like sailing on a spring breeze; badly managed they can be like flowers tossed in running water and swirled hither and thither.

The more open and casual our emotional standpoint, the more unrestrained our behavior and the more lonely and empty our spirit becomes. It is like money in a bank: the creator gives everybody the same amount but the more we spend and the more extravagant we are, the less is left. When we have spent it all we are on the road to ruin.

Follow Destiny and Treasure It

Looking on affinity as important and treasuring it is part of Zen. Affinity is the meeting and coming together of people. From the point of view of the doctrine of the origin of causes, affinity both waxes and wanes. There is gathering and dispersal. Failure to understand this principle leads to attachment and to taking the wrong road. Understanding it allows you to face affinity properly, to give it importance and to treasure it.

Here is a well known fable.

Who Was It Who Buried You
in Your Former Life?

There was a scholar who had a good relationship with a girlfriend. The pair loved each other deeply and had fixed the date of their marriage. On the day of the wedding, however, she suddenly accepted a proposal from somebody else.

After this blow the scholar fell ill. His family's many attempts to help all came to nothing. When he was at his last breath and on the point of death, a Zen master passed and learning of the situation, determined to enlighten him.

Approaching the bedside, The Zen master took out a mirror and asked the scholar to look into it.

The scholar saw a vast stormy sea with waves breaking on the shore. The body of a girl lay on the shore. A figure passed, looked at the girl, shook its head, sighed and passed on. Another figure appeared, looked at the girl and unable to bear it took off its jacket and covered her. A third person appeared and, seeing the girl, wept uncontrollable tears of sympathy. He found a shovel, dug a grave and gently buried her body.

After the scholar had seen these three scenes, the Zen master turned the mirror so that he could see the other side. In it, the scholar saw his fiancée wearing a red veil in the bridal chamber on her wedding night with her jubilant bridegroom.

The scholar looked in the mirror startled: how was it that the bridegroom so resembled one of the figures from the other side of the mirror?

The scholar was puzzled by the mystery of it and was deep in doubt when the Zen master enlightened him and said: "The body of the girl that you saw on the shore was your fiancée in a previous existence. You are the second of the figures that passed by, the one that gave her your jacket, so that in this life she had to repay your compassion by loving you, becoming your girlfriend and being with you for a while. However, the one that she had to repay with a lifetime was the one who buried her, the one who is now her present husband."

The scholar was enlightened, leaped from his bed and was cured in an instant.

Plant melons and melons will grow, plant beans and beans will grow. As you give so will you receive. Once the scholar understood this, he blamed himself for not giving as much as her present husband had and accepted the consequences in good heart.

Seeing Beauty through the Eyes of Zen

When Zen masters meet an attractive woman they always maintain their composure.

Questions and Answers
on Feminine Attraction

A Zen master asked his disciples: "How should you confront feminine attraction?"

The first disciple replied: "I would live as a hermit in the mountains and where in that life would I meet a woman?"

The Zen master replied: "Though your eyes may not behold attraction there would be attraction in your mind and even if you hid, beyond distance, higher than the moon, would that solve your problem?"

The second disciple replied: "If I saw it, I would treat feminine charm as if it were a skeleton of dirty, frightening white bones. In that way I could not become attached to it in my mind."

The Zen master replied: "If the desire in your mind has not been extinguished, even if you see a skeleton you will feel it prettier than a peach. How can you not cling to it then?"

The third disciple replied: "With no attraction in the eye, seeing is not seeing."

The Zen master replied: "When clearly there is attraction and yet to say there is none, when clearly you see and yet to say 'invisible,' is that not to deceive oneself and others too?"

The fourth disciple replied: "As a wooden figure looks without feeling upon birds and flowers what hinders us from doing the same with everything that surrounds us?"

The Zen master replied: "In that case what is there to distinguish you from unfeeling plants, trees and stones?"

The fifth disciple replied: "Attraction is

attraction and I am I. To see that which should be seen, where then is the hindrance to seeing? To avoid that which should be avoided, where then is the hindrance to avoiding!"

The Zen master said: "Excellent! Excellent!"

"Attraction is attraction" does not deny the existence of feminine charm nor abolish the beauty of women. "I am I" while appreciating and admiring feminine charm is not susceptible to seduction and preserves an attitude of detached calm. This is the key to the shedding of burdens.

"Seeing that which should be seen," appreciating when appropriate and not recoiling in disgust: avoiding that which should be avoided, transcending when appropriate and not letting the mind follow circumstance. These two are the *samadhi* of matter and void with which practitioners of Zen face feminine charm.

Great Love Forges Deep Feeling

The deep feeling of Zen is Great Benevolence and Great Compassion. Benevolence is joy, the bestowal of happiness. Compassion is the eradication of suffering.

Zen's unconditional bestowal of happiness on all sentient beings is unqualified benevolence and the experiencing of the suffering of all sentient beings as if in one body is Zen's empathetic compassion.

Commonplace love is based on the me-self and has physical pleasure as its aim. Zen's love is a great love, sublimated beyond mere self, an absolute love for all sentient beings. It is the love of "If I do not descend into hell, who does?" and a love dedicated to humanity.

The Zen master Jing Xu, a man whose mind was filled with great love, practised its essence.

Master Jing Xu

One evening, Zen master Jing Xu brought a young woman back to his room, closed the door and stayed and ate with her.

His disciple, the sutra master Man Kong, fearing that his master's reputation would be damaged if news of this matter got out, placed himself on guard at the door and put off those who came looking for the master with excuses such as "the master is resting at the moment."

But this plan could not last long and Man Kong summoned up his courage and went in. The moment he was through the door he saw a woman with hair to her shoulders lying on the bed. Slenderly built, the skin of her back was fine and white. She was beautiful and Man Kong saw with his own eyes that the master was stroking her, as natural as you please.

As soon as he saw what was happening and unable to bear the sight any longer, the disciple rushed forward and said loudly: "Master, isn't what you are doing going to injure your reputation? How are you going to justify yourself in front of those tens of thousands who hold you in such respect?"

Without a trace of anger Master Jing Xu quietly said: "In what way am I not fit to be an example?"

The disciple pointed at the girl on the bed and said in a voice of condemnation "Just look!"

With a very level voice Master Jing Xu said to his disciple: "No, you look!"

Because master and disciple had been talking to each other, the girl on the bed had gradually turned round. The disciple looked and was filled with horror. The face he saw was not the beautiful fairy-like face that he had imagined but a rotted face without nose, eyebrows or the corners of the mouth. The girl was a leper, a mad woman who was looking at herself as if she didn't know whether to laugh or cry.

The master held out the pot of ointment in his hand to the disciple and simply said: "Now, it's your turn!"

The disciple at once knelt in shame and said: "Master! You can see that which we cannot see and can do that which we cannot do. Your disciple is truly stupid and ignorant!"

It is only by transforming life's everyday feelings into a love for all sentient beings that there can be any rise in the levels of our life.

* * *

The indulgent cravings of today have dropped us into a quagmire of physical desire but Zen emotion can provide a solution that can purify the self:

When there is affinity treasure it well and possess it in happiness; when affinity dissolves, face it calmly and accept it; it is destiny (*karma*) that was gained and destiny that was not gained; meeting is destiny and so are mistakes! Destiny comes and goes and cannot be forced, nor need it be forced.

In emotional life, give more and dedicate more. Do not always be thinking of gain and possession.

The highest realm of Zen feeling is to sublimate one's own emotions into a warm love that is dedicated to all sentient beings.

Zen feeling will always be the pure land of spiritual life.

Chapter XIV
Seeing Wealth through the Eyes of Zen

There are contradictory views about the Zen attitude to wealth. One view is prejudiced towards "empty" and mistakenly believes that Zen advocates a poverty leading to asceticism. The other is prejudiced towards possession and mistakenly believes that Zen advocates the acquisition of wealth at all costs, leading to a sort of hedonism. Both these points of view are some distance away from the actual Zen concept of wealth.

The Evil of Money

The modern economy is prosperous and affluence widespread. Most people are busy racking their brains to work out how to acquire as much as possible. We work hard at our jobs, for our families, and to acquire more wealth just for the sake of being better off.

In fact, when we have no money we are troubled and worried about our livelihood; but after we have become possessed of great wealth, does happiness then drop from heaven? How many people are there really, who living a well dressed and well fed life of luxury, are convinced that they have found happiness at last?

There are many successful businessmen with property worth millions or billions who cannot enjoy even the basic pleasures of life: they cannot sleep well in their luxurious houses, have no appetite for gourmet food and, in the midst of a lavish lifestyle the envy of many, they experience no feeling of happiness.

Yet there are others whose material conditions are very basic but who manage to live a happy and fulfilled life.

What is the reason for the existence of these two completely different situations? It is because if we have greed in our hearts, we are never satisfied and are always anxious to possess more, even if we already have a great deal. On the other hand, those who want little and are easily satisfied experience happiness even in the simplest of lives.

In the Zen classics, money is a harmful snake.

Money Is a Poisonous Snake

When the Buddha was on earth and begged for a

living, Ananda was his closest attendant. One day when they were begging, they had completed half their journey and passed a ditch.

The Buddha saw something, turned to Ananda and said: "Ananda! A poisonous snake!" Ananda looked and also said: "Poisonous snake! O Revered One!" They continued talking as they walked back.

At the time, a father and his son were working in the fields and hearing of the snake ran across to look. One glance and the pair of them started jumping with joy. What snake? What was in the ditch was plainly a pile of gold. Full of joy, father and son took the gold home.

Once they had the gold they took a piece to the goldsmith's shop to exchange it for cash. The goldsmith, seeing that they were poor, became suspicious and secretly reported to the authorities. Father and son were soon arrested and the rest of the gold was discovered during a search of their house. According to the law of the time anything discovered beneath the ground became the property of the king. They were convicted of the theft of royal property and condemned to death.

At the place of execution, the father suddenly

thought of something and said to his son: "That truly was a poisonous snake!" The son looked at his father and said: "Just as the Revered One and Ananda said, it truly was a poisonous snake!"

The official supervising the execution heard this exchange and was curious and reported to the king. The king listened and asked them the origin of their conversation. They then told him of their meeting with the Buddha in the fields that day. The king thereupon released them and father and son escaped a calamity.

In real life, examples of the harm of the poisonous snake of money are too numerous to mention.

According to Zen, wealth itself is neither good nor bad in nature. The crux of the matter is whether or not you are wise in handling it. If you become a slave to wealth there is no happiness to speak of: when you become its master, wealth can add to the happiness of life.

Wealth Has Significance

When wealth is treated and managed with wisdom it is a manifestation of individual ability and also a force for progress and prosperity in society.

Eastern and western sages and philosophers have defined both their anxiety about money in the service of mankind and the behavior needed to acquire wealth through proper means and aims.

Guanzi (7th century BC) said: "When the granaries are full, then is the time for manners" suggesting that the satisfaction of basic material needs precedes consideration of other matters such as morality.

The *Analects of Confucius* said: "All men desire wealth and position, but if it is not acquired with virtue it is useless."

Again, "In the moral state, poverty is a matter for shame. In the state without virtue wealth is a matter of disgrace."

The early 20th century German political economist Max Weber pointed out in *The Protestant Ethic and the Spirit of Capitalism*:

> Through the success of their daily lives people can demonstrate to the world that they are God's chosen people. This success is the ceaseless acquisition of wealth and the more they acquire the more successful they are.

Taking this view, the more wealth we acquire the better qualified we are to be one of God's chosen people. This view influenced a considerable development in capitalism.

Buddhism and Wealth

The significance of wealth is defined in Zen. In the *AndhaSutta*, Sakyamuni divided mankind into three:

First, blind in both eyes: those without wealth who were unable to distinguish morally good from morally bad.

Second, one eyed dragons: those who had the eye for money but lacked the one for virtue, who knew how to increase their wealth but not how to develop moral qualities.

Three, both eyes open: people with eyes both for money and morality who knew how to increase wealth and how to develop virtuous qualities.

The fact that the Buddha regarded those without wealth and not those without spirit as blind in both eyes is obvious. Zen approves the principled value of money and is deeply aware of the widespread and natural view that "sufficiency in food and clothing precedes ceremony." The Buddha was very clear that these were basic demands for humanity, but that even the hungry should not extravagantly demand that they should have higher spiritual goals.

Seeing Diamonds with the Eyes of Buddha

How does the practitioner of Zen manage money properly? In the sutras, Sakyamuni directed that annual income should be managed by dividing it into four:

First, current expenditure, daily outgoings.

Second, savings against emergencies.

Third, investments to produce growth.

Fourth, charitable donations.

This fourfold division is a feasible way of managing money even today.

The Charity of the Zen Practitioner

Charity is the basic method by which the practitioner of Zen manages money. The practitioners of Zen deliver all sentient beings from difficulty and actively establish enterprises that benefit all, particularly charitable enterprises.

There are two main meanings to charity: the first is financial and material charity; the second is the charity of the word of Buddha, spiritual charity.

A successful man said: "By continuing to acquire more wealth, although I may have no need of it myself, I can use it to help those who have real need." Equipped with a loving heart and the wisdom of Zen we can, at the same time as benefiting ourselves, benefit others and society as a whole through charity.

The value of money lies in its use. In the end, the successful entrepreneur becomes a philanthropist. An entrepreneur is somebody who moves wealth around society, from one member to another. That hard-won wealth, more than one can spend, should be contributed to benefit society. The money is not ours. This is why people say that we earn money during the first half of our life and give it away in the second. Since it must be given away whether we like it or not, why not be happy and generous rather than miserly and miserable?

What is well off? Sometimes we think that being well off is to have money, and that when we have the most money we are the most well off. However, in the actual world, a person is never well off when he has the most money but when he is able to give to others.

Boundless Wisdom

The material wealth of the world is not inexhaustible. Only spiritual wealth, wisdom, is inexhaustible.

We pursue material wealth but we should pursue

spiritual wealth all the more. This is what Zen calls the virtuous wealth of the word of Buddha, Zen wisdom.

We speak of fixed assets and portable assets. In fact, fixed assets only enjoy relative stability, real estate may depreciate, fittings may be damaged and their useful life limited.

Thus, when we are in business and acquiring wealth we should not just look at our gains but also consider what we have lost, otherwise we shall find that in making limited material gains we have become life's greatest loser. Like throwing pearls to catch a magpie, only when we have caught the magpie do we realise that what we have lost far exceeds the value of the little that we have gained.

If the making of money cannot add to the happiness of life, then what uses can it have?

It can buy food and clothing but not satisfaction;

It can buy medicine but not health;

It can buy surroundings but not the mood in which to enjoy them.

If you were to ask whether there was anything that could be called a lifetime fixed asset the answer would indubitably be wisdom.

The Sound of Laughter from the Bean Curd Shop

There was a rich man who labored mightily each

day with knotted brow and pursed lips but could never raise so much as a smile.

Next door there was a bean curd shop run by a young couple from whence the day-long sound of singing and laughter reached the rich man's house.

One day, the rich man could stand it no longer and went round to the bean curd shop where he found the young couple laboring wearily away.

With sudden sympathy the rich man said: "You seem so over-worked that you can only raise your spirits by singing. I would like to help you live a really happy life."

He then put down a large amount of money and left.

That night the rich man lay in bed thinking: "Now that the young couple need no longer laboriously make bean curd the sound of their laughter will be even louder."

Next morning however, there was no sound of singing from the young couple, nor was there on the second and third mornings. The rich man was perplexed and decided to go and find out what had happened.

At that moment the young owner of the bean curd shop saw the rich man and hurriedly said:

"Sir, I was just looking for you. I want to return your money."

"Why?" The rich man asked.

"Before we had this money we worked very hard making bean curd to sell and although it was hard work we were free of anxiety. But once we had the money neither I nor my wife knew what to do for the best. Should we go on making bean curd or not? If we didn't, where was our actual happiness? If we go on making bean curd we can support ourselves and what should we do with so much money?

If we have it at home we are frightened it may get lost and we have neither the ability nor the interest to do business with it. So reckoning backwards and forwards we hadn't the heart for laughter. So I'm giving it back to you."

The rich man had to take back the money, but in the morning he heard the sound of laughter from next door.

* * *

When money manages man it is a poisonous snake that brings disaster to countless families; but when we manage money with wisdom and use it to serve us it can create happiness.

The Zen attitude to money is one of earn, spend and worth. Doing business earns money that must then be spent. There is a limit upon what can be spent upon oneself. Spending charitably upon those who need it most makes money play its best role so that it can enrich individual happiness by several thousand-fold. This kind of life is significant and worthwhile.

Material wealth is limited but spiritual wealth is without limit. Mankind's most treasured wealth is wisdom and spiritual joy its greatest happiness.

Chapter XV
Tea and Zen Taste the Same

The Zen master Yuanwu's saying that "tea and Zen taste the same" has been part of China's cultural history since ancient times. We frequently hear expressions in daily life that indicate a connection between tea and Zen. For example "go take tea" which relates to a Zen *koan* of the Tang dynasty Zen master of Zhaozhou, and "harmony, respect, purity and tranquillity," the four most important elements of the tea ceremony. Zen tea culture has had a major influence on the Chinese people's attitudes towards life up to the present day.

There is Zen in a bowl of tea. It enshrines the *samadhi* (Zen concentration) of life and the aspirations and good taste of the tea expert.

Entering a world fragrant with tea and heavy with the scent of Zen, to taste and appreciate a bowl of tea can make one's life a little calmer and a little more at ease.

Causes of the Success of Tea with Zen

Tea has three qualities: it prevents drowsiness and keeps you awake so that seated Zen can be performed through the night without falling asleep; it helps the digestion; it can suppress the Seven Emotions (joy, anger, sorrow, pleasure, love, hate, desire) and Six Cravings (the sexual attractions of color, form, bearing, voice, smoothness and countenance) and prevent an explosion of desire. Because of these three qualities and their similarity to the principles of Zen, tea very much conforms to the moral concepts and lifestyle of Zen practitioners. Greed can be eradicated through the practice of Zen and life lived more purely and tranquilly.

In the mid-Tang dynasty, the Zen master Bai Zhang formulated *Bai Zhang's Rules of Purity*. Thereafter monastery etiquette concerned with tea became more and more standardised. For Zen, the dignified taking of tea became a serious practice.

The Tea Ceremony

Lu Yu of the Tang dynasty was known as the "sage of tea." He wrote the *Classic of Tea*, the first more or less comprehensive work on the subject. In it he wrote "the flavor of tea is cool and is suitable for drinking by those who are virtuous of character and simple in habit." Later, "virtuous of character and simple in habit" became the epitome of the Chinese tea ceremony.

The monk Jiao Ran, a friend of Lu Yu, mentioned the "way of tea" in his *Songs of Tea*: "Whosoever comprehends the way of tea is pure in character," meaning that the tea ceremony preserves man's original purity of character.

Lu Yu's *Classic of Tea* established the outward form and philosophical principles of the spirit of the tea ceremony and the poetry of Jiao Ran gave the tea ceremony its name. It manifests the intellectual content and spiritual taste embodied in the act of drinking tea, and through cultivation of both character and nature elevates thinking to a realm rich in philosophical principle.

Tea skill comprises the techniques, rules and methods of tasting tea; tea art is the manifestation of tea skills through the artistic recreation of the historical circumstances of tea drinking.

Go Take Tea

The "go take tea" *koan* of the Zen master Zhao Zhou (778~897) is probably the most classic of all Chinese Zen tea *koan*.

The Zen master Zhao Zhou who was in

charge of the Guanyin monastery at Zhaozhou in Hebei, asked a recently arrived pupil: "Have you been here before?"

The pupil said: "No, I haven't."

The master said: "Go, take tea."

The Zhao Zhou master then asked another pupil whether he had been there before. The pupil replied that he had and the master said: "Go, take tea."

The temple master did not understand this and said: "Whether they've been here before or not been here before, you, sir, tell them to go and take tea?"

The Zhao Zhou master loudly called: "Temple master!'

"Uh!" responded the temple master. The Zhao Zhou master said: "Go, take tea."

At first sight, this thrice repeated "go, take tea" *koan* of the Zhao Zhou Zen master appears to be a simple triple repetition of the phrase. In fact, however, it incorporates a Zen philosophical device of limitless mystery.

Within a pot of tea lies the unlimited appeal of life. But one bowl alone is not sufficient to allow you to appreciate life's true nature and significance. However much you learn, it is all without substance. It is useless to know facts by the multitude but to be unable to do anything. It is useless if you cannot put Buddhist thought into practice, though you may be conversant with thousands of Buddhist *gatha* (verses) and know all the sutras by heart. Zen incorporates theory with the practicalities of the present day and into life. That is something of real use.

Green Tea Is a Meeting of Minds

Tea experts have always placed great importance on the quality of Zen tea. A bowl of green tea is an encounter with nature and with the wonder of one's own true nature.

The character for "tea" (茶) is formed by "man" (人) between "grass" at the top and "tree" (木) beneath, that is to say man in the midst of nature. In the midst of nature there is no need for man to wear the mask that he normally does in society. This is when his spirit is at its most natural and he can allow his original mind and true nature to manifest themselves and he can feel exceptional love and friendship.

To return to the world of plants is to return to the world of green willows and red flowers—nature as it was.

Green Willows and Red Flowers

Murata Shuko (1423-1502) was the originator of the Japanese tea ceremony. At the age of 19 he entered the Jyuan temple (the present Ikkyu temple) of the Daitoku monastery of the Rinzai school in Kyoto. Shuko studied with the Zen master Ikkyu, whose *dharma* he received.

Shuko was uneasy because he frequently fell asleep but was cured by drinking tea.

One day, Zen master Ikkyu asked him: "In what state of mind should one drink tea?"

Shuko replied: "One drinks tea for the sake of one's health."

Ikkyu asked further: "A pupil once asked the Zhaozhou master what the essentials of Zen were and he replied 'go, take tea.' What is your view of this *koan*?"

Shuko was silent and Ikkyu asked an attendant monk to bring Shuko a bowl of tea. Shuko had just taken the tea bowl when he heard Ikkyu give a great shout as he knocked it from his hand.

Shuko did not move an inch, made an obeisance to Ikkyu, stood up and said farewell.

As Shuko reached the door, Ikkyu suddenly called to him to stop and said: "Just now, I asked you what was to be gained from drinking tea. Now, shall we talk not of that but just of the drinking of tea?"

Shuko calmly replied: "Green willows and red flowers."

Ikkyu smiled with satisfaction and bestowed his *dharma* upon him.

Thus, Shuko amended his understanding of tea drinking: drinking tea had nothing to do with health or hobby, even less with research into tea art, for it had already strengthened his mood of enlightenment.

A bowl of tea contains all the experience of life.

What do green willows and red flowers mean? They mean that every natural object exists in its own original state. Willows are green through the state of being green, and flowers red through the state of being red. There is no later conceptual intrusion or interference. It is only by returning to the state of the original, to the point where a consciousness of the relative had yet to appear, that we can achieve a relaxed and healthy mindset.

This is a lifelike manifestation of both the true original spiritual state of nature and of our own original spirit.

The Unity of Internal and External

The environment of the tea ceremony is formed by a combination of the internal and external. The internal achieves unity with the external when the internal and external environments of the tea ceremony are pure and free from the dust of the mundane. At this point, one can enter a state of tranquil spirituality, return to the pure origins of "green willows and red flowers" and experience the spirit of "harmony, respect, purity and tranquillity."

Purifying the Mind

One day, Sen-no-Rikyu (1522-1591) attended a tea ceremony held by a tea master early in the morning. On entering the tea pavilion, he saw that a few fallen leaves lay scattered on the floor, giving it a rustic air. Sen-no-Rikyu turned to the guest behind him and remarked: "Such an elegant atmosphere but our host today is of limited cultivation. I'm sure he's bound to sweep these leaves away."

During an interval in the ceremony several guests again assembled in the pavilion. As was to be expected the pavilion had been swept clean and not a leaf was to be seen. In respect of the host's unremitting efforts Sen-no-Rikyu then pronounced: "As to the sweeping of the pavilion court, if the ceremony is early in the morning it should be swept during the night: if the ceremony is at midday then it should be swept early in the morning. Once swept, even if leaves do float down, they should be ignored and nature left to take its course."

To sweep leaves away once they float down is an affectation and rigidly over-particular. It results in the destruction of the natural atmosphere.

I once tasted tea at the Purple Bamboo Forest on the top-most peak of the Zhongnan Hill near Xi'an, as well as at the Pinshan pavilion of the Jingye temple there. Enjoying the elegant mountain scenery and sipping the fragrant tea I came to comprehend the sense of nature that surrounds the tea ceremony. As I tasted the tea in those surroundings I felt that heaven and earth had become the tea pavilion, that the Big Dipper was the spoon, that all creation was the guest and that the wind in the pines was the sound of the *qin*, sending my soul wandering to the ends of the universe, so that between neither knowing nor feeling I entered a spiritual state of purity.

Harmony, Respect, Purity and Tranquillity

Harmony, respect, purity and tranquillity are the spirit of the tea ceremony.

Harmony: A Bowl of Tea Holds Harmony

Harmony is at the core of the philosophy of the Chinese tea ceremony. It is a philosophical principle common to Confucianism, Daoism and Buddhism.

The Confucian idea that "Harmony is noble" is the basic ethos of the Chinese people. The harmony of the tea ceremony complements the harmony of the *Book of Changes*. The harmony of the *Book of Changes* refers to the way in which all the constituents of the universe are formed by the two basic elements of Yin and Yang. Only if Yin and Yang are in balance can there be a universal principle for mankind.

Daoism also places great importance on the role of harmony, believing that strong and weak are complementary, that the seasons should be in balance, that spring should bring forth and summer grow, autumn gather and winter store in a single canvas of harmony.

Harmony is an extremely important concept in Zen too. It could be said that the practice of Zen is performed in order to achieve harmony. Zen believes that mankind's troubles derive from ignorance and stupidity. Trouble and vexation are caused by the struggle within the mind between opposing concepts. This is disharmony. Through the practice of Zen it is possible to transcend the concept of opposites to reach happiness of mind. This is the summit of Zen and supreme enlightenment.

The concept of harmony also plays a substantial part in the tea ceremony.

Lu Yu's *Classic of Tea* mentions a "wind" stove used for making tea. In 1988, just such a stove was amongst the tea utensils excavated from the underground palace of the Famen Temple. The stove was made of iron, hence "gold"; its fuel was charcoal, hence "wood"; the stove made tea, hence "water"; the charcoal burnt, hence "fire"; it was placed on the ground, hence "earth." Thus the process of making tea included the five elements of gold, wood, water, fire and earth in mutual interaction and eventual harmony.

From the point of view of appearance, the "equal pourer" used in the tea ceremony is the ultimate expression of the principle of harmony.

When making tea the usual practice is to pour the tea from the pot into the equal pourer. If tea is poured directly into the bowls, the first bowl is clear and weak and the last is thick and bitter. Consequently, tea from the same pot can contain all the differences between clear and weak and thick and bitter. The equal pourer, however, has an adjusting function so that the tea that it pours is of the same flavor however many cups are poured.

Respect: The Sada Aparibhuta Bodhisattva

The *Lotus Sutra* contains a figure called the Sada aparibhuta bodhisattva who saluted whoever he met with respect and said: "I hold you in the utmost respect and harbor no feelings of disrespect. Why? Because no matter how you feel at present, in the future you will achieve enlightenment and become a Buddha, so I have the deepest respect for you!"

In the tea ceremony, the treatment of others with respect is regarded as extremely important.

Sen-no-Rikyu was once invited to taste tea by a man called Chikuan. At the time, Sen-no-Rikyu was the foremost tea master in Japan and of considerable fame. Chikuan was delighted that Sen-no-Rikyu was to appear and believed that it gave him face. When Sen-no-Rikyu and his disciples entered the tea room, Chikuan personally poured tea for them.

However, because of his excitement Chikuan's

hand trembled, the bamboo teaspoon fell to the ground and the tea utensils were nearly overturned, a veritable chapter of accidents. So far as the fluent, graceful performance of a tea ceremony was concerned Chikuan hardly counted.

The disciples sneered laughingly behind their sleeves.

By contrast, Sen-no-Rikyu's reaction was completely different. At the close of the tea ceremony and as principal guest he praised his host saying: "Sir, your pouring of tea today was the best beneath heaven!"

The disciples failed to understand their master's intention and when they returned to the monastery they asked: "The host at the tea ceremony today nearly broke all the bowls. Master, with such unsuitable pouring, why did you say that it was the best under heaven?"

Sen-no-Rikyu said: "It was because that out of respect for us, our host was over excited. In the tea ceremony this respect for others is of the utmost importance. What would it have mattered even if he had overturned the tea utensils? You should know that in the tea ceremony, this spirit of respect is much esteemed."

Purity: The Six Purities

The "purity" of the tea ceremony refers to the gleaming state of purity of the external material world and of the inner mind. In this context external purity extends from the sprinkling and sweeping of the pavilion courtyard to the sweeping of the tea room and its decoration. For example, flowers should be fresh and the cloth used to clean the tea bowls should be new.

At the same time, the mind should be cleansed and without impurities. At this point, the eye should see an environment of purity, the ear should hear the water boiling in the kettle as the sighing of the wind in the pines, the nostrils should inhale the wonderful fragrance of tea, the tongue should taste its refined flavor and the body should feel the elegance of the utensils. This is the way to acquire a sense of tranquil seclusion. These are the six purities.

In this way, though seated in a tea room of only a few square feet, there is a sense of being deep in the mountains. The mind becomes completely dissolved into a unity with nature. This is the *samadhi* of tea and the *samadhi* of Zen.

Tranquillity: Once in a Lifetime

The "tranquillity" of the tea ceremony is Nirvana, the serenity that comes after the fires of desire have been extinguished. It is the mood of contentment, the dampening of the flames of vexation and the attainment of purity and enlightenment.

The extinction of desire is the Zen mind of tranquillity. Nevertheless, this mind is not a stagnant pool of water, since the person who has achieved enlightenment is filled with love and arduously revisits the clamor of the world of dust to work diligently for the salvation of all living things. This is the mood of "all embracing love is the Zen mind" that belongs to the tea ceremony.

This profound feeling is expressed in the tea ceremony as a mood of "once in a lifetime" (in Japanese, *ichigo ichie*), originally a phrase from Japan's Warring States period indicating that we should bring the whole of our body and mind to the drinking of the bowl of tea before us. It is one of the tea ceremony's major ideas. "Lifetime" means the whole life of man and "once" that there is but the one opportunity. There are countless encounters during a lifetime but no guarantee that they will happen again.

"Once in a lifetime" is a reminder that we should treasure every passing moment and that since this might be our only chance, we should make every effort. If, through indifference, we neglect what is before us we may regret it for the rest of our life.

Life gathers and disperses, disperses and gathers, no

meeting is ever the same. Not only is it difficult to meet close friends, it is even more difficult to encounter one's true self, so that one should redouble one's efforts to treasure what there is.

Through our inborn character, the "harmony, respect, purity and tranquillity" of the spirit of the tea ceremony represent universal virtues: the virtues of moderation, respect in all we do, purity of character, and tranquillity of mind and body. This is the highest state of self-cultivation achieved by the Confucians, Buddhists and Daoists of traditional Chinese culture. Through the tea ceremony, Zen is a model for contemporary spiritual life amidst the turbulence of life today.

* * *

Finally, I have some words of blessing for everybody:

First, the heart in a leaf of tea.

"Man betwixt tea's grass and tree, happy to dedicate himself for all. Braving fire and water, to lift the spirit of mankind."

I hope that all those with affinity will live in this world with the heart that lies within a leaf of tea. What kind of tea leaf is this? If we look at the ancient tea masters, despite being between tea's grass and tree (a reference to the incorporation of the character for "man" within the components of the character for "tea") their position was limited and they had little influence on society. Nevertheless, they were happy to dedicate themselves to others and devote themselves to all sentient beings, to brave fire and water for the spirit of all. As the tea leaf simmers in the water, and heats on the stove, this is its mission, its final destination. It sacrifices its identity in an act of self-dedication so that everybody may enjoy a perfect spiritual life. This is also the mission of each of us in life.

Second, the three teas of life.

China has many different kinds of tea—green tea, Wulong, black tea—but each kind has its own flavor. Life, too, has many flavors but the highest is the realm without flavor.

When we are young we are full of longing for life, and for romantic passion. At this point, the tea is sweet in flavor. In middle age the flavor may be a little bitter, a little astringent. The ripe wisdom of old age transcends the flavors of sour, sweet, bitter and hot, transcends thick and clear and reaches a flavor that is without flavor, the ultimate flavor of all. These are the three teas of life. In each stage of life it will be enough to seek to enjoy them.

Taste pure tea with an ordinary heart, nurture an

ordinary heart with a pure tea.

The mystery of Zen is concentrated within a mere bowl of tea. This is known as: there is no second flavor to tea and Zen, a bowl of pure tea can intoxicate.

Chinese Titles of Texts

Copyright © 2013 Shanghai Press and Publishing Development Company

This book is edited and designed by the Editorial Committee of *Cultural China* series

Text: Wu Yansheng
Translation: Tony Blishen
Cover Image: Quanjing
Interior Designer: Wang Wei
Cover Designer: Diane Davies

Copy Editor: Diane Davies
Editor: Zhang Yicong
Editorial Director: Zhang Yicong

Senior Consultants: Sun Yong, Wu Ying, Yang Xinci
Managing Director and Publisher: Wang Youbu

ISBN: 978-1-60220-141-5

Address any comments about *Chinese Zen: A Path to Peace and Happiness* to:

Better Link Press
99 Park Ave
New York, NY 10016
USA

or

Shanghai Press and Publishing Development Company
F 7 Donghu Road, Shanghai, China (200031)
Email: comments_betterlinkpress@hotmail.com

Printed in China by Shenzhen Donnelley Printing Co., Ltd.

1 3 5 7 9 10 8 6 4 2